"As a member of the senior White House staff and a veteran in banking and the executive search fields, I have interviewed thousands of highly successful people. In *Run With the Bulls Without Getting Trampled*, Dr. Tim Irwin nails the essential differences between those who do well and those who don't. If you want to know what it takes to make it in any endeavor, read this book!"

—J. Veronica Biggins
Senior Partner, Heidrick & Struggles

"Dr. Tim Irwin has been a trusted advisor for many years. I respect his advice because he has both the educational background and the business experience to really understand people. *Run With the Bulls Without Getting Trampled* is a practical book because he tells what a person must do to and how to make the changes that lead to success. I strongly recommend this book!"

—William B. Johnson
Founder, Ritz Carlton Hotel Company

"Dr. Tim Irwin has the proven depth of experience and leadership in the arena of senior executive development. He has overseen the development and execution of our most successful senior executive development program. He knows what senior executives need to run a $70-billion dollar company, and now he's put his knowledge and experience into this great book!"

—Brian Fishel
Senior Vice President, Executive Development, Bank of America

"Dr. Tim Irwin, a longtime friend, amazed me when I learned he ran with the bulls in Pamplona, Spain. This adventure as well as a number of others serves as hard-hitting metaphors, which he brilliantly melds into the most enjoyable business book that every CEO should read. He leaves out the stale corporate jargon and puts in well-crafted, heartfelt, experience-based business principles for those who really want to succeed at work. I'm giving this book to every CEO I work with!"

—Mac McQuiston
President/CEO, CEO Forum, Inc.

"Dr. Tim Irwin is a valued senior advisor. His unique ability to bring solutions to an organization's toughest problems is extraordinary. I'm glad to see his principles in print."

—WILLIAM H. GRUMBLES, JR.
President (ret.), Worldwide Distribution, Turner Broadcasting System, Inc.

"Because I worked with Tim Irwin for a number of years, I know he understands both the theory and realities behind organizational behavior. Changes he helped design in my organization continue to bear fruit even a decade later. It is a testimony to his guidance that the backbone of that organization still remains after numerous reorganizations and being acquired by another company. *Run With the Bulls Without Getting Trampled* is filled with foundational principles that set apart strong leaders—leaders who truly care about their organizations' long-term successes. The stories and anecdotes make the principles easy to remember and will inspire both new and experienced leaders. It's a must-read!"

—HELEN MIYASAKI
Site Director, Clariant Life Science Molecules, Inc.

"It takes more than just hard work to achieve the greatest business successes, and Tim Irwin understands this definitively. *Run With the Bulls Without Getting Trampled* touches upon many elements of the depth and breadth of what it takes to make a truly seasoned—and effective—leader, no matter the industry. As a leader of the world's largest casual dining company, I found the message of this book incredibly relevant and absolutely valid."

—CLARENCE OTIS
Chairman/CEO, Darden Restaurants, Inc.
(Parent Company of Olive Garden, Red Lobster,
Smokey Bones, and Bahama Breeze)

"As someone who has worked in a family business since age nine, I realize that success is born out of adaptability and self-transformation, and Dr. Tim Irwin makes this point and many others with great impact. You will be captivated by his stories, which he links to critical principles of success in business and the reality of life in general. If you're engaged in the process of building your business or career, I highly recommend *Run With the Bulls Without Getting Trampled*."

—DAN CATHY
President/COO, Chick-fil-A

"To be effective, strategy must be well executed by great people. Tim Irwin knows what makes people great in the workplace. In my twenty years in the corporate world, *Run With the Bulls Without Getting Trampled* captures the essence of true success as well as any book I've read. What really sets this book apart is how well these principles are conveyed. Irwin's fresh perspective and personal stories make this a wonderful read!"

—MARJORIE DORR
Chief Strategy Officer, WellPoint, Inc.

"In *Run With the Bulls Without Getting Trampled,* Tim Irwin draws from twenty years in the marketplace to distill the attitudes and disciplines needed to thrive in your current work environment. With humor and highly relevant cultural examples, Irwin's knowledgeable approach will help you identify your own objectives and transform them from mere aspirations into realties. I underlined, circled, and dog-eared my way through every chapter. Great job, Tim!"

—ANDY STANLEY
Pastor and author

"The post-modern world rejects truth and moral absolutes. But Dr. Tim Irwin exposes the fallacy of this—by showing that when people go to their workplace, they discover that life only functions with meaning when it conforms to reality, that is, truth. This is a very significant book presented in a readable fashion—lots of storytelling and good illustrations—but it's the message that is powerful and makes the book important reading for anyone who wants to find meaning in the workplace."

—CHARLES W. COLSON
Founder/Chairman, Prison Fellowship

"For the past two decades, Dr. Tim Irwin has had a distinguished career as an organizational psychologist, consulting with many of the world's most successful organizations. We can now benefit from his experience and glean what he has learned about people who thrive and falter in the workplace. This is a stellar book, and anyone reading it who aspires to succeed with integrity will benefit from Dr. Irwin's wisdom and insight."

—GARNETT S. STOKES, PH.D.
Dean, Franklin College of Arts and Sciences, University of Georgia

RUN
WITH THE
BULLS
WITHOUT GETTING TRAMPLED

RUN
WITH THE
BULLS

without GETTING TRAMPLED

THE QUALITIES YOU NEED TO STAY OUT OF
HARM'S WAY AND THRIVE AT WORK

TIM IRWIN, PH.D.

NELSON BUSINESS
A Division of Thomas Nelson Publishers
Since 1798

www.thomasnelson.com

Published in Nashville, Tennessee, by Thomas Nelson, Inc.

Published in association with the literary agency of Wolgemuth & Associates, Inc.

Nelson Business titles may be purchased in bulk for educational, business, fund-raising, or sales promotional use. For information, please e-mail SpecialMarkets@ThomasNelson.com.

Scripture quotations from The Holy Bible, New International Version®, Copyright © 1973, 1978, 1984 by International Bible Society, used by permission of Zondervan Bible Publishing House. All rights reserved.

Scripture quotations from The Message by Eugene H. Peterson, Copyright © 1993, 1994, 1995, 1996, 2000, 2001, 2002, used by permission of NavPress Publishing Group. All rights reserved.

Scripture quotation from The Living Bible, Wheaton, Illinois, Tyndale House Publishers, 1971, used by permission.

Library of Congress Cataloging-in-Publication Data

Irwin, Tim, 1949-
    Run with the bulls without getting trampled : the qualities you need
to stay out of harm's way and thrive at work / Tim Irwin.
        p. cm.
    Includes bibliographical references.
    ISBN 0-7852-1951-X (hardcover)
1. Success in business—Psychological aspects. 2. Commitment
(Psychology) 3. Integrity. 4. Performance. 5. Work ethic. I. Title.
HF5386.I66 2006
650.1—dc22
                                                    2006021425

Printed in the United States of America
07 08 09 10 11 QWM 5 4 3 2 1

To Anne, Jim, and William,
who have made life a great adventure!

CONTENTS

SECTION 3

EXCEPTIONAL COMPETENCE

FOREWORD

R*un With the Bulls*—it caught my attention the moment I looked at the cover! And once I began to dig into the book, I realized Tim and I shared a common bond—a framework that expresses the many years of experiences observed in successful leaders.

Like many students of leadership, I have kept a living and working description of what makes individuals successful that has shaped my own journey. I have been privileged to work with and for many great role models; as a result, my personal model of leadership has morphed over the years as I learned from them. They have helped to mold who I am as a leader.

During the past five years as CEO of PepsiCo, I have shared those personal principles with young leaders in the company. What truly captivated me about Tim's book was that he somehow took many of the same experiences I have observed, and even taught, and expressed these characteristics in a way that better reflects my thoughts than I have been able to do myself.

His 3C model (Commitment, Character, Competence) is a wonderful and holistic way of capturing almost everything that I have valued in leadership. These three words stand alone like a good political cartoon in the editorial section of a newspaper that gives a concise visual description of a detailed editorial.

Tim does a great job of explaining these three attributes. His seven critical success factors define what it means to be competent and are an excellent way to really put truth into his principles in a personally penetrating way. You can feel your own successes and failures in the examples and questions that are so well crafted they come to life on the pages.

It has been my experience that developing a model for leadership and success in an organization is a helpful exercise and provides for interesting talks, but the real issue becomes, what do you do about it? This book encourages you to formulate your own thoughts about these characteristics and validate them with your experiences, and then do something about it.

Change is hard, particularly for people who have been very successful in parts of their lives but are not complete and satisfied with their whole lives. Having a change model and a specific tool to effect that change is critical. Tim provides that tool.

Run With the Bulls Without Getting Trampled is a great book for anyone who is a student of leadership and wants to be successful in today's organizations, but it may be most helpful for those who are in the early stages of their careers—young leaders who are beginning their search for a significant life.

I identify with Tim in a number of ways, but maybe the most important one is that two of my four children are in their twenties, and they are well on their way toward a significant life. I am excited about having my oldest sons read this book as they complete their preparation to *run with the bulls!*

—Steve Reinemund
Chairman & CEO, PepsiCo

PREFACE

In my first real job I sold shoes at a shopping mall near my family's home. It was pretty straightforward. Measure the customer's foot and find the correct size in a particular shoe. Put it on the person's foot and talk about the positive attributes of the shoe. You can learn a lot about people through their feet, but I'll spare you the specifics.

Mr. Randolph, my manager, taught me how to sell shoes, but he didn't say much about *work* and how to do it well. None of my teachers, parents, coaches, or the other important people in my life ever gave me a handbook on how to work. My dad was a great role model, but he never explained to me how to be really successful at work.

Even at a young age, I instinctively knew how consuming a role work plays in our lives. It confused me that for most people walls separated their work and life. Many seemed to work so that they could do what they really wanted to do. In my shoe store, everyone lived to get off from work—life happened outside the store.

Without question, work is one of the most dominant dimensions of our lives. Most of us spend more than half of our waking hours working, so it's a huge commitment of our life energies, especially when you multiply those many hours by forty, fifty, or even sixty years. By some estimates, we will spend over 100,000 hours at work in a lifetime.

Although I am still fairly young by many standards, I have already worked for about forty years if you count my lawn service at age eleven.

If we define work as "what we labor at," then the definition broadly includes almost everyone—for example, a corporate executive, an assembly-line worker, a teacher, a stay-at-home parent, a plumber, a surgeon, a nun, an attorney, a pilot, a volunteer leader, a waiter, a coal miner, a minister, or thousands of others in the workplace. Our work so dominates our waking hours that it's hard to imagine how we can be successful at life without being successful at work.

Our work so dominates our waking hours that it's hard to imagine how we can be successful at life without being successful at work.

Unfortunately for so many, work is not what we relish but rather a major source of pain. Wouldn't it be wonderful to say at the end of our lives, "That was worth it—the challenges, the hardships, and the rewards. I didn't randomly career through forty years of work in confusion and distress. I invested those years well. I made a difference. The many thousands of hours I spent at work were successful and significant." How can we learn to work this way?

As a corporate psychologist, I have met with thousands of leaders and individual contributors, many of whom were highly successful in their respective organizations, each with their own remarkably individual stories. I have also made a career-long study of the relationship between the work and the worker. This book will provide you the distilled essence of my own experience and the experiences of all those intriguing people I've interviewed—the spirited core of many deep conversations about their work and their lives.

While experts may not agree in every detail, a fairly broad consensus exists as to what attributes make people effective in their chosen work. My research supports these broad findings. I have also learned that many who are judged to be successful are not satisfied—they have not found personal meaning in their work. I learned that those who succeeded and found significance in their work, regardless of their specific occupation, had these qualities:

Thoughtful Commitment
Authentic Character
Exceptional Competence

Ultimately, *Run With the Bulls Without Getting Trampled* is about personal transformation. How can you grow to your fullest potential and become someone who will spend those forty or more years until retirement working for meaning, not just money? The three qualities above are the essential, foundational elements of success and significance. A number of important attributes are grouped under these three main headings, and a summary at the end of each section recaps the big ideas covered.

While knowing what has made others successful may be interesting and possibly even personally relevant, it doesn't necessarily answer the question of how we develop those attributes in our own lives. Despite a deep longing to be different and repeated efforts to change, many fail to become the person they want to be.

Candidly, I write out of a background of struggling deeply with personal change. In my twenties, I found myself adrift and unsettled. I had friends, got by in college, and stayed busy, but life had very little clarity. My life was like turning the focus ring of a camera backwards and forwards, trying to get a clear image. I desperately needed a basis for making important decisions, such as what type of work to pursue, whom to marry, how to spend my free time, where to live, and which friends to have.

Two life-changing events proved to be emotional wake-up calls. First, a very serious dating relationship dissolved. In hindsight, I discovered that I was adrift in life *and* in the relationship. I had no vision—no great purpose to join up with and nothing significant to accomplish with a soul mate.

Over a period of several years, a second wake-up call occurred more gradually when I heard a number of different speakers who had profoundly impacted the world in their sphere of influence. Their consistent challenge to pursue a life of significance became a clarion call for me to commit to something bigger than simply filling up twenty-four hours a day. They were not asking me to join a cult and move to South America but to pursue significance in every aspect of life: in my studies, my future career, and my relationships. Both of these experiences proved to be catalytic events in my life and formed the backdrop of much that I will express in this book about how to be effective in the workplace.

I changed the details in many of the numerous workplace illustrations to protect the privacy of others; however, the personal stories in each chapter are true. My intent was to convey the very important information in this book in an entertaining manner, so you will see that I learned some critical lessons about work and life the hard way.

ACKNOWLEDGMENTS

I want to thank all those individuals who have shared their stories with me during the last twenty years—a wonderful tapestry of talented and highly motivated leaders and individual contributors. What I learned from them formed the foundations of this book.

Although envisioned for many years, when the time was finally right for writing *Run With the Bulls Without Getting Trampled,* an amazing group of advisors appeared. My close friend and colleague for more than two decades, Pat MacMillan, gave his time and ideas with extraordinary generosity as the concepts for this book began to take shape. His insightful feedback about various stages of the manuscript was crucial.

I am truly fortunate to have as my agent the person whom many experts consider to be one of the best in the book publishing industry, Robert Wolgemuth. Robert's willingness to represent me was a tremendous encouragement. Time and again his wise insights have proven invaluable.

I've also had the privilege of working with two outstanding editors. Brian Hampton incisively identified the substantive issues I needed to address to make this book work, and Paula Major skillfully managed the process of transforming the manuscript into a book.

Thanks to Nicola Russell, who perceptively read my manuscript through the lens of how best to communicate with the audience I sought to reach; Kevin Small, a very savvy man, who freely shared his insights on writing books in the twenty-first century; and Dr. Gail Wise and Dr. Amy James, who were tremendously helpful in organizing and implementing the online assessment and developmental resources.

Special acknowledgment goes to Anne, Jim, and William, without whom the great adventure would not have happened. Those three and now dear Elisabeth and McKenzie formed the chorus of encouragement to tell the story.

1

THE RUN

*In bullfighting they speak of the terrain of the bull
and the terrain of the bullfighter. As long as a bullfighter
stays in his own terrain he is comparatively safe. Each time
he enters into the terrain of the bull he is in great danger.*
—ERNEST HEMINGWAY, *THE SUN ALSO RISES*[1]

The smell of livestock and damp hay hung in the Spanish air like humidity after a summer thunderstorm. The scent wafted over the freshly washed streets. Despite that morning's hosing down, the worn cobblestones still felt slippery from the stale beer and wine spilled by revelers the night before, mingled with who knows what else. But as the crowd of men standing in the street grew, the acrid smell of body odor sharply displaced the other aromas.

Along the winding cobblestone street, centuries-old three-story buildings with wrought-iron balconies were covered with flowering vines almost as vivid as the runners. Up and down the street, large throngs of noisy spectators leaned over the balconies and stood on nearby walls to watch the unfolding spectacle. The muted voices of other runners standing around in small groups grew in intensity as the start time approached. Suddenly, quiet prevailed as the men in the street spontaneously burst into a beautiful song, a prayer to the city's patron saint. "We ask San Fermin to guide us in the bull run, giving us his blessing."

We were all dressed alike—runners in the official uniform of San Fermin—white shirts and pants, with long red sashes tied around our waists and red bandanas around our necks. Many of the men looked worse for wear after a long and sleepless night of drinking and carousing. Some, in their dirty, wine-stained suits, looked like they had slept curled up in an alleyway. We were the *corredores* running in the *encierro*, trying to safely reach the *Plaza de toros*—the runners in the fenced-off street sprinting to the circular arena or bullring. For the *corredores* standing in the street that morning, running in the *encierro* was a badge of honor and a rite of passage. Some runners learned to be *corredores* as young boys, trained by their fathers with the kinder, gentler bulls on the opening day of San Fermin. All experienced a kinship with the brave *corredores* who had run before them in summers past.

The city of Pamplona was named after Pompey the Great, a Roman general who occupied the colorful Basque city around AD 75. Ernest Hemingway memorialized Pamplona and the festival of San Fermin in his novel *The Sun Also Rises*. The festival, which is held each year in the second week of July, honors the first bishop of Pamplona, who was martyred for his faith in Christ. While San Fermin has become a rowdy, drunken, eight-day carnival, at its heart it is still a religious celebration honoring this third-century saint. The red scarves we wore, called *pañuelos*, symbolized the shedding of the saint's blood.

During the day, the city vibrates with color and sound. Beautiful horses, resplendent with silver-clad saddles and bridles, carry riders in shimmering costumes reminiscent of sixteenth-century festivals. With bells clanging, the horses that are used to drag the carcasses of bulls killed by matadors parade through the cheering spectators. Loud bands march around the city with large, gaudy religious figures suspended on tall poles. Throngs of partyers in their red-and-white outfits roam the narrow streets, drinking wine morning and night from leather wineskins called *botas*. The excited children and oversized puppets dancing in the streets are like Disney World the week after schools recess for summer. The sidewalks bulge with the tents of vendors hawking their wares—red sashes, bandanas, and every other form of memorabilia. Bright table umbrellas crowd the sidewalk cafes at every plaza, and each night after the bullfight, a brilliant fireworks display showers the city. Every afternoon, matadors fight and kill the bulls that ran in that day's *encierro*. The costumed matadors' artful flair, the magnificent horses, the stern officials overseeing the event, and the 60,000 cheering, booing, and singing fans rival any NFL playoff game for bravado and pageantry.

Most foreigners know San Fermin simply as "the running of the bulls." On each of the eight days of the festival, six bulls and six steers are released from a pen at 8:00 a.m. The steers run alongside to calm the bulls in the roaring crowds. They also guide them through the winding 800-meter course through the center of the old city to the bullring. In preparation for this event, I learned that a bull weighing 1,400 pounds could run 100 yards in six seconds, besting even the fastest Olympic sprinters. Bulls are big, fast, aggressive, territorial, in-your-face, and have a permanent bad attitude. Anything moving gets their attention. Their spirited nature causes them to lower their horns and charge anything or anyone in their way. The bulls run the winding and narrow street from the bullpen to the arena much faster than any of us on two legs. Grave peril awaits anyone in the bulls' paths. All *corredores* feel a sense of angst—will the bulls' horns find them today?

For my son and me, running with the bulls was one of those ideas that started on a lazy Saturday afternoon grilling steaks on the deck. My younger son, William, idly mused, "It might be fun to run with the bulls." We discussed this possibility in the safety of our backyard, purely from a theoretical perspective. But over time, our decisionmaking took small incremental steps until suddenly the accumulated momentum swept us along into doing something we would never have considered in a single rational moment. William, who was going to Spain for his second summer of language study, made the notion much more intentional. "Dad, why don't we run with the bulls *this* summer?" When I sensed William's seriousness, my concern for his safety compelled me to join him. So that's how we ended up standing in a narrow European street with 1,800 other white-suited, red-sashed runners waiting for the sound of a bottle rocket to announce that we had better run for our lives.

Have you ever read about one of those soccer games where the crowd panics and people get crushed in the stampede? I had never appreciated how the force of people running away from something could be so powerful. When this fairly mellow gathering of friendly people saw the bulls charging up the first hill, they instantly turned into a mob of completely self-absorbed individuals intent on personal survival. This mixture of adrenalin, testosterone, and fear was the most overwhelming force I have ever experienced.

This mixture of adrenalin, testosterone, and fear was the most overwhelming force I have ever experienced.

That morning our destination was clear—the arena. The plan was simple, logical, and straightforward: run up the hill to the plaza 100 yards ahead, move over by the fence, climb over the fence if necessary, let the bulls pass by, and then follow them into the bullring. We would focus on staying out of the bulls' way and not getting tangled up with any of the other half-crazed runners.

Military planners often say that no battle plan works out as intended after the first shot is fired. Remember that fence we were going to climb? By the time we arrived, it was seven-deep in people with the same great idea, and there was no sign of an opening. The only thing I remember is the strong arm of my middle linebacker son, wrapped around my chest to drive me into the crowd along the fence. I barely had time to turn my head to see twelve huge animals with wide, pointed horns zipping by us within spitting distance.

A runner 50 yards ahead of us was not as fortunate. One of the bulls in the lead knocked him over without breaking stride. We were all told that if you fell down, the cardinal rule was to stay on the ground until all the bulls passed by. I knew that if I went down, I was going to cover my head and get into a fetal position. This young man decided to get up and move to the side. As he stood, another charging bull knocked him down. Incredibly, the same runner tried to stand up one more time! As we watched the slow-motion video replay later that day, the runner looked like a quarterback blindsided by a blitzing linebacker penetrating the line untouched—knocked into the air, his back arched and his head snapping backwards. TV commentators during the live broadcast actually gave him high marks for raw courage and style but low marks for judgment.

Despite all the fanfare, the running of the bulls is over in less than five minutes, as the bulls and runners reach the inside of the arena. Among the several thousand runners, a number are injured each day, some seriously. During the week that we ran, there were sixteen runners gored by the bulls, the highest number recorded in twenty-five years. Fifty-six runners were taken to the hospital. Eight of the gorings happened on the same day with a particularly aggressive group of bulls. The injured included a doctor from Atlanta who was gored in the groin. Some runners trip or fall over other runners and are trampled, receiving bruises, concussions, and even permanent brain damage.

Being gored by a bull plays into our worst primordial fears—the thought of a huge, mindless beast driving his horn into your back generates a good shudder when you ponder it for a few seconds. Hemingway observed and wrote about the first recorded death in the *encierro* in 1924. In his scene, the main character learns of the runner's fate; a waiter comes to his table and says of the young father named Vicente Girones, "You hear? Dead. He's dead. With a horn through him."[1] The bull that gored him was named Bocanegra. In the story, a matador fought and killed Bocanegra that afternoon during a bullfight in the *Plaza de toros*, the same arena we ran to during our *encierro*. Since 1924, twelve runners have died. In 1995, Matthew Tassio from Glen Ellyn, Illinois, died after a bull's horn pierced his back, stomach, and liver, severing an artery. After being knocked down, Tassio violated the cardinal rule of "once down, stay down." He stood up and was subsequently gored to death. This young American was a recent college graduate on a summer trip to Europe with his friends.[2]

> *Running with the bulls is a very clear metaphor for our lives at work—a race filled to the brim with challenges, opportunities, and even dangers.*

My sons and I have been on many hair-raising adventures, such as scuba diving through ocean caves and rappelling off thousand-foot cliffs near Yosemite National Park, but redundant safety systems and experts on hand always mitigated the dangers and assured that we were safe. Pamplona was different. We signed no releases of liability freeing the city fathers from responsibility. This was not a roller coaster with a predictable ending. We simply stepped into the street and waited for the bulls to be released, hanging onto our rough semblance of a plan.

Why would anyone in his or her right mind participate in such an event? I will attempt to answer that question later in more detail, but for now I want to point out that running with the bulls is a very clear metaphor for our lives at work—a race filled to the brim with challenges, opportunities, and even dangers.

The bulls in Pamplona were not out to get us. They're territorial and aggressive but not mean. They were indifferent to our presence . . . unless we got in their way. They didn't run out of the pen looking for someone to gore, but it is in their DNA to use their horns on anyone encroaching

> *An organization's goals are extraordinarily simple and straightforward—survival and success—and to not meaningfully contribute to these goals (or even to be irrelevant to the accomplishment of them) automatically puts us in harm's way.*

on their space. It would have been naïve to assume otherwise. They were indifferent to our hopes and dreams, and they couldn't have cared less whether or not we reached the stadium. The bulls' aggressiveness was simply their nature, and that predisposition only became apparent when they were kept from accomplishing *their personal goal*—to get out of the bedlam and munch on some nice grain in a quiet place.

The bulls serve as useful symbols for everything that creates the context of our work lives—the events, the circumstances, and the obstacles. "Bulls" constantly rage around us in the workplace. Inept managers, downsizings, misguided compensation systems, constant churn, outdated IT systems, ill-designed prcesses or structures that make our jobs difficult or even obsolete—they're all part of normal organizational life. To view these organizational realities as unfair or out to get us is impractical and maybe even naïve. These "organizational bulls" are indifferent to us (unless we get in their way), ultimately not caring whether or not we reach our goals, *but rather whether or not they reach theirs.* An organization's goals are extraordinarily simple and straightforward—survival and success—and to not meaningfully contribute to these goals (or even to be irrelevant to the accomplishment of them) automatically puts us in harm's way. As Hemingway points out, "Each time he [the bullfighter] enters into the terrain of the bull, he is in great danger."[3] An organization's survival and success are the terrain of the bull.

One of the savviest CEOs I've ever worked with often said that he was never surprised when people or organizations acted in their own self-interest. Even companies that strive to be the "employer of choice" in their market or to have a supportive, uplifting culture do so out of self-interest. We should not be surprised that organizations make decisions to assure their own success and survival. Even most bad decisions are fundamentally motivated to help a company succeed—the decisions were just misguided.

All organizations constantly seek to achieve their owners' expectations. Even if drastic measures are required, achieving the next quarterly earnings estimates or being able to assure stockholders that the company will remain in business another year is a nonnegotiable in today's business environment. Even nonprofit organizations, whose mission is usually altruistic, still seek first and foremost to remain in existence. While an effective individual manager may care about our hopes, dreams, and aspirations, the *events* swirling in and around an organization do not. The organization's only focus is achieving its goals, and an organization seeking success and survival will trample us if we do not run skillfully.

These organizational bulls won't be tamed or go away and are not going to get less dangerous. We might even make a case that the bulls have become more dangerous in recent years. Some of our fears—such as terrorism, job loss, porous borders, and economic uncertainty—are felt more intensely than ever before.

Our work life—the focus of this book—is a run with the bulls, replete with both opportunity and danger. Some of us work skillfully, navigating through and around the danger, while others are repeatedly knocked down. The expression "getting ahead" is a race metaphor that describes how many of us strive to get a bigger job, with more power, more money, and a more significant title. Many senior executives even have "coaches." An executive coach's role is to help a manager perform his/her job more effectively and to realize his/her potential for more responsibility in leading the organization—to get ahead.

We all know people who are getting ahead, others who are falling behind, and some who never got started. A few run with their organization's bulls skillfully—they have good insight into the omnipresent politics in organizational life and just seem to know what to do. They're able to get things done; to work well on a team; to get along with their boss, their peers, their subordinates, and their customers; and to get what they want from the organization. Others bounce from company to company or from job to job, unsettled, searching, and constantly in turmoil.

Many people live soap-opera lives, careening from one intense moment to the next, never having really satisfying work relationships. We know people who live from paycheck to paycheck with credit cards maxed out, skirting one financial disaster after another and never getting on solid footing. These trends can often be spotted early in life. Others finish school, get responsible jobs, and live productive lives. A few never seem to get it together. These hapless casualties may not even know they're in a race and never even get to the starting line. They have problems from the start, fall behind, and become dejected spectators rather than participating in one of life's great races. Perhaps they were the victims of a teacher or a bully and then later a boss, disgruntled customer, or some other obstacle ostensibly not of their own making. More likely, they lacked purpose and direction, compromised their character, or failed to develop the critical competencies so essential to compete in the twenty-first century.

And then there are the posers. In San Fermin, they wore the white uniform, and pretending to be brave, they ran in the street—but at a very safe distance from the bulls. They began the race near the arena. Long before the bulls arrived, these runners simply jogged into the stadium. They immediately became the objects of derision of the fans waiting in the stadium and were pelted with debris for arriving early. They were not really engaged in the run. They talked the talk, but didn't run the run. You and I know people who do not really engage work and life in a serious way. Perhaps afraid, these individuals show very limited initiative and take no risks. Nothing of significance emanates from their lives. They show up for work but dwell constantly in the twilight of obscurity, usually rated the benign "satisfactory performer" on their annual performance appraisal.

We are in the race whether we want to be or not. We must run with the bulls skillfully to avoid getting trampled, gored, or repeatedly knocked down. This requires great wisdom and forethought—we must develop a strategic mind-set. We must also run the race with many other anxious runners who are intent on trying to win their own race. Some are skillful, and some are not. Some have integrity, and some do not. A few selfishly elbow you out of the way or knock you to the ground to accomplish their goals at your expense.

Donald Trump's popular TV show, *The Apprentice*, serves as a transparent microcosm of what goes on in the race of work and life. The premise of this "reality" show is that only one of the bright, attractive, young aspirants will win the race and make it to the top to work for Trump's corporation. One or more participants get fired each week, and the backbiting and maneuvering during the various tasks becomes Machiavellian almost beyond description. The cameras carefully document the manipulation and deceit of the participants. The final boardroom scene, during which Trump pronounces who leaves the show that week, is the ultimate judgment on who has run the race well and who has run the race poorly. The now infamous line, "You're fired," brutally condemns the loser. The bravest and most secure among us know that the outcome of the race always remains in doubt. We worry ourselves sick when we are repeatedly knocked down—bloodied, bruised, and even out of the race.

During the half-mile run with the bulls, each runner makes many choices in order to stay out of danger. In many cases, a different choice would have made an enormous difference in preventing an injury. What is especially painful are the people who make the same mistakes over and over, just like the runner who unwisely kept getting up, only to be knocked down by another bull. They refuse to learn from experience.

In my twenty-five years of consulting in the areas of leadership development, performance management, and career planning, I observed a pattern. Individuals who build successful careers with purpose and significance consistently display a pattern of critical attributes. The chapters ahead explore these qualities and define both their meaning and importance in helping us stay out of harm's way and thrive in the world of work.

Both of my sons played college football, and as they neared the end of their respective careers they became philosophical about the game. My favorite axiom from these two wise men is, "Football is simple, but it's not easy." I think we can say the same thing about running the race set before us. Running the race well and avoiding danger is much more about perspective, common sense, and getting along with others than it is about knowledge and intelligence. There are practical skills to help us make better choices. In fact, knowing what to do in most cases is simple—it's just not easy.

> *Individuals who build successful careers with purpose and significance consistently display a pattern of critical attributes.*

Note to reader: To view a video of our run with the bulls, go to runwiththebulls.net

Thoughtful
Commitment

Significance • Intentionality

2

RUN TO WIN

Every man dies, but not every man really lives.
—BRAVEHEART, PARAMOUNT, 1995

His sweat-drenched hair against my face, I held my son as his body shook with heaving sobs. The game, the season, the countless predawn weight-room sessions and two-a-day practices . . . the investment of eight years of his young life all came down to one Friday night. As cocaptain, he had devoted everything to inspire this team of young men to surpass everyone's expectations.

Earlier that evening, an electric atmosphere warmed the chilly December night. It was true Norman Rockwell Americana—lush green turf with perfect white stripes brilliantly illuminated, animated cheerleaders at their practiced best, bands blaring, and the intense pregame warm-ups anticipating the epic battle about to unfold.

This was no ordinary game—it was the third round of the high school state football play-offs. The teams' energy quickly transformed the waiting crowds into a fever-pitched frenzy—both sides desperately wanting their team to prevail. I was the proudest dad on the planet as I watched my son walk out to midfield for the coin toss.

An epic battle it was. Neither team really lost that night, even though the opposing team had more points on the scoreboard and advanced to the semifinals. Behind by two touchdowns at the half, our team fought back fiercely, almost tying the game in the closing minutes.

When the final seconds had ticked off the scoreboard clock, the families walked on to the field to meet the heartbroken players. I held my inconsolable son, and the tears streaming down his swollen, bruised face captured what we all felt—the bitter disappointment of losing and the sadness felt by twelve seniors and their families. This would be the last of their "Friday night lights."

As steam from his overheated body rose into the cold night air, the head coach of the opposing team walked across the field directly toward us. He turned to me and said, "Sir, may I speak with your son?"

I moved away as he put his hands on my son's shoulders and looked directly into his reddened eyes. Barely audible to me, I heard the coach pay this young player the supreme compliment. "Son, tonight you left nothing on the field. You gave it your all, and it was an honor to play against you." At that, he turned and walked the length of the field to the end zone, where his celebrating team drowned out the other sounds of the night.

Isn't this what we really want someone to say at the end of our game, "You didn't leave anything on the field—you gave it your all"? As George Bernard Shaw so eloquently wrote:

I want to be thoroughly used up when I die, for the harder I work the more I live . . . Life is no "brief candle" to me. It is a sort of splendid torch which

I have got hold of for the moment, and I want to make it burn as brightly as possible before handing it on to future generations.[1]

Aristotle observed that every person is drawn by a *telos*, a purpose or goal. Sometimes a movie, speech, symphony, sunset, professor, minister, or even a manager at work awakens that longing for purpose and significance. I believe that, deep down, all of us want to know that at the end of the game, we gave it our all in pursuit of high and noble ends . . . to have a deep sense of significance in our lives.

Just as there are moments when our need for significance is uniquely awakened, there may be long periods in which we feel hindered in our pursuit of anything high and noble. Numerous realities of life are capable of draining the vitality from our need for significance. The list below includes some of the most powerful ways by which we thwart our pursuit of purpose and meaning.

A LIFE OF QUIET DESPERATION

Early in my practice as a psychologist, a man from the Midwest in his late forties with an Ivy League education sat down in my office and graphically announced that he had the "whore and the Harley syndrome." When I asked him to explain, he told me that he hated his job and felt confined by his life commitments. As the founder of an avionics manufacturing company, he couldn't leave his CEO responsibilities at the office—they followed him everywhere. His schedule of business, community, and family commitments was grueling. He also had a big mortgage, four kids in private schools, and a beautiful but very expensive high-maintenance wife. He disparagingly called it the "commitment life"—a life full of commitments to others. My client lamented that what he really wanted was "to get a whore and a Harley and go to California!"

As we talked further, I learned that my client, although exceptionally talented, began to drift into what was now a "life of quiet desperation" in his early twenties. His self-focus resulted in a vague and unintentional life trajectory leading him nowhere in particular. He was tired of the commitment life, which included the big mortgage in the gated community but mainly required him to constantly serve his family and be responsive to the needs of his company's employees. He admitted that he just wanted to be twenty-two again and have fun—he longed for the freedom of youth. In his hopelessness, he contemplated an illusory return to freedom—abandoning his family and business commitments for a perfect storm of certain disaster.

According to a January 24, 2005, *Time* magazine article titled "Grow Up? Not So Fast," a whole new generation of young adults called "twixters" is questioning the "commitment life" of their parents. The article suggests that their commitment to just about everything—apartments, jobs, and relationships is fleeting. Lev Grossman writes, "There was a time when people looked forward to taking on the mantle of adulthood. That time is past. Now our culture trains young people to fear it." One twixter quoted in the article said, "I don't ever want a lawn, I don't ever want to drive two hours to get to work. I do not want to be a parent . . . why would I?"[2]

It would seem just the opposite, but commitments don't confine us. They liberate us from a life of self-absorption. At the end of people's lives, they don't celebrate how much money they made (or left behind), how many gated communities they lived in, how many relationships they had, or how many video games they mastered. They celebrate the hard things—serving others, being steadfast and faithful to a life partner, raising a healthy and accomplished family, persevering and overcoming difficult circumstances. This kind of life often requires that we put others' needs ahead of our own, but at the end, we will have "burned the torch brightly."

COMPLACENCY

Dictionary.com defines *complacency* as, "A feeling of contentment or self-satisfaction, especially when coupled with an unawareness of danger, trouble, or controversy." Complacency undermines commitment, because we're lulled into a false contentment. We feel self-satisfied, calm, content, and tranquil, but it's unwarranted. It makes us passive. Our initiative dries up, and we cease taking purposeful steps toward a meaningful end.

"Smells Like Teen Spirit," a top-of-the-charts song from the rock group Nirvana, contains a memorable lyric: "Here we are now, entertain us." With a whole life and an ocean of opportunity before them, many frame the boundaries of their planning horizons by what they will be doing two hours from now. Their job is something they muddle through between weekends. And who can blame them? It's so easy to default to a self-satisfied inertia that these individuals never get really clear about where they're going with their jobs or their lives. A life of significance requires focus, intentionality, effort, and forethought. Complacency and resulting passivity keep us from being thoughtful about where we're going in life.

Many are like Alice in Wonderland, who asked the Cheshire cat which direction she should take. "'That depends a good deal on where you want to get to,' said the Cat. 'I don't much care where,' said Alice. 'Then it doesn't matter which way you go,' said the Cat."[3]

If we want to get somewhere in particular, it does matter where we go and which way we walk. Life is

For many, living has become more important than life.

the consequence of the choices we make. Complacency is a decision to let circumstances and events control us. It's like a car pulling a trailer down a mountain. If the driver is not careful, gravity can cause the trailer to go faster than the car pulling it. When that happens, the trailer rocks violently and pushes the car, in many instances causing an accident. The solution is counterintuitive—the driver must not step on the brakes to slow down but on the gas to speed up so that the car leads the trailer. When circumstances and events are in control, they push our lives toward danger and destruction. The solution is to reassert control in our lives. We must get out in front and decisively drive our lives forward with clarity of purpose.

THE DAILINESS OF LIFE

A primary reason many people don't pursue a life of significance is that they are too busy providing for themselves and their families. Life is so *daily*. Most of the people we know spend their energy coping with life in its most rudimentary form. Getting up and going to work, taking care of a family, having a few friends, and paying the bills are about all most people can handle. And then, when you add an unexpected crisis such as the teacher conference for your underperforming child or the septic line backing up, the wheels come off. For many, living has become more important than life. Whatever dreams they might have had are crushed by the demands of just keeping up. The thought of abandoning oneself to a high and noble purpose seems more than overly idealistic. And if it is ever to be considered, it must be later—"after things have quieted down and I have had a chance to catch up."

Typically the biggest challenge in daily life is our job. Maybe this describes you. It's easy for work to become a means to an end—just a way to pay the bills. Working this way precludes any opportunity to see a connection between your life direction and what you spend 50 percent or more of your waking hours doing.

Perhaps you're feeling like your time is being wasted by inept managers or chewed up by competitive colleagues. It's hard to have high and noble thoughts when your coworker stabs you in the back and makes you look like a fool in front of your boss. I spoke with a highly successful young manager recently who said, "I don't like the person I have to become to be successful here." Another frustrated worker told me, "Our corporate culture is to constantly beat people down until they conform."

A lack of connection between our personal mission and our job often leads us to resent the demands placed on us even by well-managed organizations.

Pressure to reach financial goals and to meet quarterly earnings expectations creates an extraordinarily oppressive and stressful workplace. Sometimes work is bone-numbingly boring, with expectations to work unbelievably long hours. The smog-enveloped traffic in the daily commute flares the tempers of even the most self-controlled. For those who travel, the security lines, long delays, and crowded airplanes grind them down to unyielding fatigue. A number of studies have shown that as many as 85 percent of Americans hate their jobs. As comedian Drew Carey quips, "Oh, you hate your job? Why didn't you say so? There's a support group for that. It's called *everybody*, and they meet at the bar."[4]

It's no wonder you see *Dilbert* cartoons posted on the walls of office cubicles. For many, Dilbert's cynicism is not parody—it's reality.

A lack of connection between our personal mission and our job often leads us to resent the demands placed on us even by well-managed organizations. We then work like mercenaries, simply paid to do a job with no real commitment to the cause. With this mind-set it is difficult to see work as a vital and primary means to achieve a life of significance.

FEAR

Fear dominates our attention and compromises our effectiveness. Fear makes us tentative, and tentativeness makes us fail.

In my work with corporate leaders over many years, I have frequently accompanied groups on team-building retreats and planning meetings. I joined one group at a beautiful mountain retreat for a leadership development exercise. I arranged for the group to be trained on a ropes course, where they were given the opportunity to experience a variety of physical challenges. The plan was that by successfully overcoming physical risk taking, these leaders could then face leadership challenges with greater confidence.

The defining exercise of the week was nicknamed the *Pamper Pole*, an instrument of torture requiring the hapless volunteer to climb a forty-foot telephone pole. On top of the pole was a small platform eight inches square on which the climber was expected to stand. The move from pole to platform gave the victim great insight into the name of the exercise and made those adult diaper commercials potentially more relevant.

Standing on the platform, their eyes were forty-six feet off the ground as the pole swayed gently in the breeze. Just when they thought it couldn't get any worse, the climbers realized that they had to dive off the platform and grab a trapeze six feet away. This part was by far the most interesting. I was about fifteenth in line, so I had the opportunity to watch the other participants. Of those ahead of me, only two reached the trapeze and held on. The rest fell and were caught by a safety rope tied to their harnesses.

These leaders exhibited four different approaches during this part of the exercise. I nicknamed the first group the *Pretenders*. They had the appropriate gear on, but they simply looked at the pole and walked away. Or at most, they climbed a few rungs on the ladder and quit.

Group two was the *Timid*, who climbed the pole and in a few cases even made it to the top. However, they took one look at the trapeze and declined to dive for it. Paralyzed by their fear, the Timid simply eased off the pole into the security of the safety rope.

The third group was the *Tentative*. They actually dove for the trapeze, but the hesitation in their dive diminished their reach. They failed to grab the bar securely, and it was jerked from their frustrated grasp.

Group four, the *Committed*, reached the bar and held on. They dove so hard that their bodies literally flew across to the trapeze. They dove with total abandon. In fact, they overreached and were able to grasp the bar with arms bent.

The Pamper Pole is a useful metaphor for how people approach their lives. The Pretenders wore the garb but didn't really get in the game. (My Texas friends would call them *Big Hat, No Cattle*.) The Timid were easily thwarted and gave up without much of a fight. Confronted with the reality of the task, they shrunk back from the challenge. The Tentative tried harder but were still cautious and irresolute. Many people you and I know approach life just trying to avoid failure, which makes them tentative. The result is a diminished chance of reaching their goal. The Committed abandoned themselves to the goal and overcame their fears. Their singular focus and resolute effort led to success where the others had failed.

Even though you may never have an opportunity to jump off a pole (or even want to), I suspect that you still know which group you're in. Commitment to a life of significance requires that we dive into our work and life with abandonment.

CONFORMITY—JUST GO ALONG

Recently, I drove to the airport and hurriedly looked for the nearest parking space. Because I hate those nasty door dings, I always try to pull into a space with plenty of room between the two cars on either side. When I finally found a space, I pulled in carefully with an eye on the cars to my right and left. As I was getting my bags out of the trunk, I noticed my car was centered between the two other cars, but it was at an angle to the white stripes on the pavement. As I looked more carefully, it became obvious that the first person to park his car that day had carelessly ignored the painted stripes, and all the rest of us had simply followed suit. I had parked in relation to those around me rather than the stripes. It was easy to do; I simply looked at the other cars and determined where I should park.

Conformity, one of the most powerful social forces in a workplace, can defeat our noblest aspirations. One reason the pressure to conform is so powerful is its subtlety. Pulling into my space was easy; I simply did what others around me had done. The white stripes were background with little practical relevance. The definitions of normal and correct were what others did. It seemed natural to go with the flow.

"My question is: Are we making an impact?"

Even if we want to pursue significance in our work life, it's still much easier to just get by—not to stand out from the crowd. Conformity rarely leads to much impact. A life of significance usually requires that we paddle upstream against the current of others' expectations or the organizational norm. The wolves in that *New Yorker* cartoon are all great at howling at the moon in exactly the same way—they're conforming to the wolf in front. They're all oriented to the moon in just the right way, all howling the same discordant notes. That's what wolves are supposed to do—right? At the risk of being rejected by the pack (being a nonconformist), one wolf finally exhibits the courage to ask the tough question—does what we're doing have any value?

COUNTERFEITS

Before returning to the US from Seoul, South Korea a few years ago, I went to a famous outdoor market, known for its knockoffs of famous brands. The stores sold everything imaginable—watches, luggage, clothes, shoes, and so forth—but many were counterfeits. My sons were in a growth phase during which they outgrew their clothes every few months, so I thought it was a great time to pick up some "designer label" shirts for them . . . cheap. The shirts looked great on the boys for one wearing, but the first time through the washer, they literally came apart at the seams. Counterfeits often look good but ultimately are proven worthless. The greatest danger of counterfeits in our lives is that they rob us of a life of significance—they look good briefly but then are ultimately proven worthless. Three examples deserve special mention.

MATERIALISM

The pursuit of money as life's chief goal is at the top of the counterfeit list. Actually, the people who focus on money are not so much in love with money but with what money can buy—power, fame, toys, comfort, and so on. In many cases, having money does make life easier and more comfortable. I have flown coach, and I have flown first class, and first class is better. But money—or what money can buy—is not what makes us happy, especially at the end of our earthly existence. Does anyone really believe that bumper sticker that says, "He who dies with the most toys wins"? I have always wanted to pull alongside and ask the driver, "Wins what?"

Regarding this subject, Gregg Easterbrook wrote in *Time* magazine:

> There is a final reason money can't buy happiness: the things that really matter in life are not sold in stores. Love, friendship, family, respect, a place in the community, the belief that your life has purpose—those are the essentials of human fulfillment, and they cannot be purchased with cash. Everyone needs a certain amount of money, but chasing money rather than meaning is a formula for discontent. Too many Americans have made materialism and the cycle of work and spend their principal goals. Then they wonder why they don't feel happy.[5]

Not long ago a very wealthy man in his mid-seventies boasted to me that he was frustrated with getting old because he kept thinking of new ways to make more money. He was greedy, and pathetic, and I wanted to tell him to get a life. What he really needed was a more noble passion—one that would endure.

CAREERISM

Another counterfeit is careerism, putting a career first above all else. Self-serving, promotion-oriented behavior is at the core of this mentality, and advancement is placed above the needs of family, friends, organization, and even one's own best interest such as health. As the *New Yorker* cartoon on the following page expresses, some people take commitment to their careers a bit too far.

"Mr. and Mrs. Stephen McCarter James request the honor of your presence at the marriage of their daughter, Deirdre Belknap, to her job."

At the heart of careerism is the idea that a job makes a person significant. What careerists often don't talk about is the price they pay personally. Stories of legendary business leaders often include their undying loyalty to the company and its mission as they sacrifice families and health to advance their career. It can be as funny as someone taking his Blackberry into a bathroom stall to respond to an e-mail or as serious as an executive's pursuit of his own advancement at any cost—usually compromised integrity.

Career advancement is a normal, expected result of succeeding in our job. We should take our jobs seriously and, as we grow in our capabilities, larger responsibilities often follow. The problem results when we make the bigger title or more money the sole objective. Performing well in our job is the means to more responsibility. When money, power, or job title is the primary goal, character-compromising means of achieving that goal are inevitable. I never cease to be amazed at the duplicity, the deception, and the deceit that some individuals exhibit when career advancement is their god. They never miss an opportunity to gain an advantage with false diminishment of the achievements of others, back-stabbing, lying, and self-promotion.

SELF-FULFILLMENT

Self-fulfillment is another counterfeit that our culture prods us to pursue. Just look at the first five ads you see in the next magazine you pick up at the dentist's office. Many people have created an art form of stringing together beautiful moments. There is nothing inherently wrong with enlightenment, beauty, education, sports, personal growth, thrill seeking, food, art, music, or travel, but when we make these or similar pursuits the main source of our significance or happiness, they prove to be counterfeits. If we enjoy these types of experiences en route to a life of significance, they can provide fun or enriching moments in our lives. The problem results from making self-fulfillment the primary reason for our existence.

In the film based on Norman MacLean's novel, *A River Runs Through It*, Robert Redford's character mournfully describes one of those fleeting peak moments as he looks down on a beautiful river raging through the wilds of Montana. His yearning is for the magnificent scene to remain like a work of art and set him free from the constraints of daily life: "And I knew just as surely and just as clearly that life is not a work of art, and the moment could not last."[6] Despite the transience of pleasure, many spend their lives in pursuit of the next overrated, contrived experience.

A related problem many people experience is "living for the weekend." Certainly, I look forward to weekends, holidays, and vacations. We typically love time off to pursue hobbies, enjoy occasions with friends and family, and find adventure, but when work becomes only the means to do what we really want to do, unconnected with any real sense of significance, then boredom, resentment, and frustration ensue. Living only for the weekend is a natural result of a lack of connection between our jobs and a clear and compelling sense of significance in our work. When our job simply pays for what we really want to do, there's a big disconnect.

Some psychotherapists and self-help gurus tell us to find self-focused ways to make ourselves happy. Paradoxically, so many people who spend a lifetime chasing self-serving ends wind up really unhappy. In reality, serving others, making a difference, and pursuing significance in our jobs make us happy. With this perspective in mind, weekends and vacations become great times to renew ourselves, but they're not what we live and work for.

A lifetime of absorption with contrived experiences to achieve self-fulfillment leads only to anguish. The main character in the John Grisham novel *The Broker* brings this to light. At sixty, the character remorsefully views his life from the rearview mirror as he drives past his old office:

> Somewhere in there, on the top floor, he'd once ruled his own little kingdom, with his minions running behind him, jumping at every command. It was not a nostalgic moment. Instead he was filled with regret for a worthless life spent chasing money and buying friends and women and all the toys a serious big shot could want.[7]

A LIFE OF SIGNIFICANCE

Even though the distractions described in the preceding pages may not fully hinder us, they remain powerful and pervasive influences in our lives. The only hope of overcoming these influences resides in a purpose that calls out to us more powerfully. It requires the discovery of an undeniably compelling purpose.

One of my favorite movies is *Saving Private Ryan*, in which Army Captain John Miller, played by Tom Hanks, leads a squad of soldiers sent out to find the last surviving son of a family who had already lost three other sons on the same day. Toward the end of the movie, as the soldiers spirit Private Ryan away to safety, they are drawn into a battle that appears hopeless. They fight heroically as they wait for reinforcements. In the closing moments of the battle, Captain Miller is fatally wounded, and Private Ryan rushes to his side. The captain strains to speak his dying words. "Earn this." Captain Miller charges Private Ryan not to waste the sacrifice made on his behalf—to live in a way that recognizes the tremendous price that was paid so that Ryan could live.

At the end of *Saving Private Ryan*, the now seventy-year-old Ryan visits Captain Miller's grave in France. We get the impression that not a day has gone by over the last fifty years during which he didn't think about Captain Miller's sacrifice for him. That another person gives up his life on behalf of Ryan redirects his life and adds a compelling dimension of seriousness and earnestness about how he is to spend his remaining years. It no doubt affects his priorities and how he spends his time. It impacts his marriage, how he raises his children, and how he works. It gives his life purpose and direction.

FINDING WORK WITH SIGNIFICANCE

Although their experience obviously differs from the fictional Private Ryan, a clear distinctive of those individuals who achieve great things is that they pursue purpose and significance with their lives. Finding purpose and significance orders our priorities, how we spend our time, how we view our relationships, how we raise our children, and *how we work*—the subject of this book. Purpose and significance create earnestness and focus.

A question that we might ask at this juncture is how do we find purpose and significance in our work?

> *Individuals who achieve great things pursue purpose and significance with their lives.*

The answer lies in the *work that we do* and the *worker that we become*, as described in the upcoming chapters. The answers in many cases are simple, but not easy.

3

THE ARENA

So watch your step. Use your head. Make the most of every chance you get.
These are desperate times! Don't live carelessly, unthinkingly.
—PAUL OF TARSUS[1]

Some years ago, a close friend and his family rented a beautiful vacation home overlooking pink sandy beaches on a turquoise bay in St. Maarten and invited our family to visit them. About mid-morning on the first day, he suggested that we rent a couple of small boats for the afternoon, so we piled into the car and drove to a local marina. Although we knew we wanted to get back to our house via the water, in reality we were not quite sure how to get there. The marina was situated on a different part of the island, separated from our bay by a rocky peninsula. When we explained to the friendly proprietor that we wanted to take the boats to the bay in front of our friend's home, he said, "No problem, mon" with his lilting Caribbean accent.

The two younger boys and I jumped into the eight-foot dinghy powered by a small outboard engine, while my friend and my older son, Jim, launched the sailboat. The erratic wind and the chattering sail did not look promising for sailing, so I threw them a twenty-foot tow rope and tied it to the back of the dinghy. After crossing several hundred yards of the inlet, we began to get a better look at the rocky point we had to get around. To our dismay, an extensive reef system with a powerful surge of crashing water loomed on the starboard side, and an endless ocean lay off the port bow. It was obvious that we needed to move away from the reef—getting caught up in the strong currents and the jagged ledges of rock and razor-sharp coral spelled disaster for the boats and for us. I looked back and yelled to my friend over the thunderous sounds of the crashing water that we needed to aim our bow to the east, which we later learned was the Atlantic Ocean. The thought of turning back never crossed any of our minds—we were men of the sea.

Have you ever become involved in something and suddenly wondered how could it possibly be happening? Now a quarter-mile offshore, without warning we found ourselves in seven- to eight-foot swells. The water had turned battleship gray, and the friendly sun of earlier that morning cast an angry glare. Gentle waves morphed into huge, frightening whitecaps. The dinghy sank down into one trough and the sailboat into another, connected only by the tugging rope. Rolling waves pushed us back toward the rocky point we desperately sought to avoid, and panic drained the color from everyone's faces. My friend and I exchanged helpless glances as he yelled against the howling wind, "This is crazy!"

Have you ever become involved in something and suddenly wondered how could it possibly be happening?

It seemed unthinkable that our circumstances could become more dire, but at that instant the engine on the back of the dinghy stalled. It was the only force providing us with any control over the giant swells, so I reached back and pulled the starter rope—it roared back to life while I attempted to aim our bow in the assumed direction of our bay, only for it to stall again. Without the engine we were directionless, surrendered to the treacherous waves pushing us toward certain injury or worse. It stalled again and again, and each time it started a cloud of gray smoke surrounded us with a choking smell from the fuel.

"Dad, I want to get in the dinghy."

"Jim, the dinghy's having trouble too . . . just hang on."

Remaining calm and focused was impossible, and the boys, silenced by their fear, squinted into the blinding sun with faces contorted by panic and nausea. Seagulls overhead mocked our plight with screeching laughter. A diabolical conspiracy between the pounding waves and the back surge from the imposing reef held our small boats with an unrelenting grip, and the ocean seemed intent on meting out a full portion of punishment for our carelessness.

In desperation, I lifted the gas tank to make sure we had fuel. As I lowered the fuel tank back to the floor of the boat, I noticed that the air valve on top of the tank looked closed. In our haste to set out, I hadn't even checked it, and I now realized that we had a vacuum in the fuel line, causing the engine to stall repeatedly. I quickly opened the air valve and prayed that the engine would keep running this time. Still totally outmatched by the conditions and dragging the sailboat through each trough, the pitiful engine labored in deep ocean swells for another hour. With painfully slow progress, we meekly worked our way home.

The boats finally came to rest on the pink sandy beach in front of the house, and we all collapsed into the nearest chairs. My wife, Anne, looked up from her book, "You guys don't look too happy. What's wrong?" No one spoke, and gloom settled over the group. Over the next few days, our ordeal was *the* topic of discussion, and the marina manager was inevitably the object of our scorn and blame. How could he have allowed us to take those small boats into that kind of water? We also learned from a waiter about a phenomenon in that area called the "Winds of Christmas." In the spring it was not unusual even on a sunny day for a calm ocean to suddenly become very rough on the windward side of the island. There we were, in the middle of a tempest, in some incredibly unseaworthy boats.

For several days, I pondered what had happened. One morning I woke up with the painfully glaring conclusion that I was really responsible for our plight—not the marina manager whom I had blamed up until that moment. I had grown up around boats and knew better. My father taught me to be a stickler for safety when on the water, and in college I received the Red Cross's highest certification—Water Safety Instructor. Based on this little stunt, they should have decertified me immediately.

It would be difficult to inventory all of the bad decisions I made on our small oceanic excursion. On a whim we had rented two boats, knowing nothing about the equipment. I didn't even check to see if the drain plug was in the boat or if the fuel tank air valve was open. I didn't verify that we had enough life preservers—fairly basic stuff. I did no planning and preparation to understand the unfamiliar route to our house. I knew nothing about the conditions. I was on vacation and feeling lazy. I wasn't there to be my usual overplanned self. As it turned out, if we had taken a different road to the marina, we could have looked down on the rocky point and seen the rough water.

SIGNIFICANCE DOESN'T HAPPEN BY CHANCE

Our nearly disastrous ocean voyage was doomed from the start. We were vague about where we were going and didn't know how to get there. We did nothing to prepare for the conditions. Our equipment was ill-suited for the journey. It was a foolproof recipe for disaster that placed one of my best friends and our three young sons in grave peril. Sadly, many are following this recipe perfectly with their careers and even their lives. They are unprepared and ill-equipped for a journey fraught with peril, treating life with the superficiality of a vacation.

Our deep yearning for a life of significance should drive us to make our work significant. Because most of us spend more than half of our waking hours working, we need to get it right. This will only occur if we're thoughtful and intentional in two areas—first, on the work that we do and, second, on the person at work we become. This chapter deals with how to choose work that guides us toward a life of significance.

How does a commitment to making our lives count guide our decisions about career? My father piloted bombers during World War II, and after the war, he flew commercial aircraft for almost forty years. Despite the many thousands of flights he made over his career, he unfailingly reviewed his preflight checklists before leaving the gate. They were his criteria for ensuring the aircraft was ready for flight. He might encounter unexpected bad weather or have mechanical problems during a flight, but he always knew that he left the airport with a sound airplane. Our jobs are a prime contributor to a life of significance, but it has to be the right job. What we need is a checklist to help us determine if we are investing our years well. What should be on our "preflight checklist" to insure that we're pursuing the right career?

PREFLIGHT CHECKLIST ITEM 1: INSPIRES PASSION

Almost every day in the small community where I grew up, a red-haired, balding man could be seen walking aimlessly up and down our main road. The man seemed harmless but always had a distressed look on his face. My mother told me that he was shell-shocked. Later, my dad explained that this man had suffered severe battle trauma during World War II and had one day snapped. "The walker," as I came to call him, never regained his emotional bearings.

This unfortunate soul provides an image of how many of us go to work. We show up and may create a lot of motion, but we have no passion or emotional focus in our work. All of us know people who are miserable in their jobs but are doing nothing about it. We have heard people say, "If I can just keep my head down for another ten years, then I can take early retirement." Have you ever heard of people who counted the days until they retired and then died within a year or two? Equally distressing are the people who retire emotionally but still come to work. They're so emotionally checked out that they haven't been truly invested in what they're doing for years. They're shell-shocked. As Homer Simpson explains to his daughter, "Lisa, if you don't like your job, you don't strike. You just go in there every day, and do it [half-baked]. That's the American way."[2]

When I was growing up, my dad would talk about his work and say, "I would do this job even if they didn't pay me." It showed—his company received hundreds of letters expressing appreciation for his work. He always took an interest in the passengers and in his crew because he genuinely cared about them. How tragic it is that more of us haven't found the type of job we can passionately care about. Instead, we find ourselves simply counting the hours until the weekend or having the "Sunday afternoon flu" every week, anticipating the dreaded Monday morning when we have to be back at work.

We should regularly ask ourselves, *Do I have this job to accomplish something significant or simply to have something to do? Am I just trying to pay the bills, or am I pursuing a life purpose that my career helps fulfill?* Having bills to pay can easily push purpose and significance lower on our priority list. Many of us had idealistic goals about what we would do with our lives as we finished high school or college, but there were numerous realities waiting to snuff out the bright candle of youthful idealism, as illustrated in the next *New Yorker* cartoon.

When we show up for work, we want to use our energy to pursue our ideals, not dream of retirement. We should all find work for which we have passion.

"I'm looking for a position where I can slowly lose sight of what I originally set out to do with my life, with benefits."

PREFLIGHT CHECKLIST ITEM 2: FITS WHO WE ARE

We were each created with a unique portfolio of abilities and personal interests. Although no job is a *perfect* fit for our capabilities, those whose personal characteristics fit their work responsibilities are in the minority. Applying our interests and abilities in the right job is deeply satisfying. Olympic runner, Eric Liddell, as portrayed in the film classic *Chariots of Fire* (Columbia, 1981), said: "I believe God made me for a purpose, but He also made me fast. And when I run, I feel His pleasure."

Many of us who are unhappy with our jobs have pursued vocations for reasons totally unrelated to our skills or passions. A lawyer told me how every day was painful because he hated his job. What he really wanted to do was teach English at a small liberal arts college. When I asked him why he didn't pursue that field, he said that he was a prisoner of $300,000 a year. After law school, his debt structure and lifestyle quickly absorbed his rapid gains in income, and the risk and complexity of changing careers were now unthinkable. Sadly, he was *working for money, not for meaning.* Some people are satisfied with a paycheck and never expect significance from their work. As Woody Allen quips, "I don't want to achieve immortality through my work . . . I want to achieve it through not dying."[3] How tragic to look back on forty years of work that were neither important nor satisfying.

Recently while having blood drawn, I sat in the special chair with the locking arm that prevents a patient from falling out if he grows faint at the sight of blood, especially his own. The young woman skillfully and efficiently prepared my arm, inserted the needle into a vein, and drew my blood. I felt no pain and thankfully said, "You're really good at this." She beamed and said, "Yes, I have a gift." Then she made the most important statement a person can make about his/her job. "I feel *called* to this work, and I help people remain calm about something that normally makes them feel anxious." We should all be so fortunate to feel called to our jobs.

> He was working for money, not for meaning.

I have a tremendous admiration for skilled carpenters, and I love to study the intricacies of fine millwork. I wish I had the innate skills to be a carpenter, but I do not. Although challenging, we must discover that vocation for which we have both gifting and passion. When we're uncertain about our interests and abilities, it may be helpful to meet with a counselor who specializes in assessing work-related interests and abilities in order to recommend the careers for which we're most suited.

What we need is an honest conversation first with ourselves and then with a trusted, candid advisor to identify our strengths and weaknesses. We need to build on our strengths and minimize the effects of our weaknesses. One woman I counseled loved animals and naturally thought about going into veterinary medicine, but in a moment of brutal self-honesty, she admitted that she did not have the scientific aptitude to get through vet school. She later decided to use her business savvy to open a unique kennel that provided a nurturing environment for pets while their owners were away. Her plan effectively built upon her strengths and acknowledged her weaknesses.

Finding a fit also means that when we're starting our careers we may have to do work that isn't completely aligned with our skills. Paying dues is normal for an entry-level position, even though none of us relish the idea of being an apprentice. Most of us would rather start nearer the top of the organization, but often the knowledge and work habits that we develop in lower-level positions are foundational for greater responsibilities.

PREFLIGHT CHECKLIST ITEM 3: SERVES OTHERS

In recent years, numerous articles and speakers have touted the idea of "Me Inc.," promoting the philosophy of putting ourselves and our career advancement first, before any concern for our company or coworkers. Tom Peters wrote in *Fast Company*, "You don't 'belong to' any company for life, and your chief affiliation isn't to any particular 'function.' You're not defined by your job title and you're not confined by your job description. Starting today, you are a brand."[4]

When we ran with the bulls, there was an overwhelming sense that every participant was attempting to survive even at the expense of others. I believe this is reflective of how many act at work.

The notion of serving others in the workplace is easy to endorse as a lofty abstract corporate value, but it is difficult to actually do. In most organizations, there is a subtle but constant game of positioning. Am I connecting with the "right" people and getting on the "in" committees? The game can get ugly. I have observed individuals trying to advance themselves in an organization at their colleagues' expense. A wronged person's first impulse is not to look for ways to serve their detractors.

The late Robert Greenleaf, a former AT&T executive, popularized a concept he called *servant leadership*, but when I use the phrase in corporate settings, I sometimes detect uneasiness on the part of my listeners. Serving others in the workplace is not normative organizational behavior and particularly does not always fit the accepted image of a strong leader. Greenleaf was right—effective leaders see leadership as a role from which to serve, not a position in which to be served.[5]

One of the most important ways a leader serves those he or she manages is to help them identify and leverage their strengths. Marcus Buckingham and Donald Clifton's research points out that, shockingly, only 20 percent of employees in the large organizations they surveyed felt that their strengths were frequently utilized in their jobs.[6] Performance management programs aimed at helping employees become more effective and productive in their roles can be a powerful way of serving, particularly if the performance conversation fosters a greater awareness of what the employee does well. Giving employees more challenging responsibilities to help them discover and develop their strengths serves the employees and the organization.[7]

> *True heroism is remarkably sober, very undramatic. It is not the urge to surpass all others at whatever cost, but the urge to serve others at whatever cost.*
> —ARTHUR ASHE (1943–1993), AMERICAN TENNIS CHAMPION

Ernest Shackleton's second expedition to the South Pole in 1914, during which he attempted to lead a group of explorers across the continent of Antarctica, is one of the greatest servant leadership stories in history. *Endurance*, the expedition's main ship, sank after being locked in a devastating ice flow for 281 days. What followed was an extraordinary demonstration of leadership, daring, hardship, and *service* to his crew. Shackleton spent a month crossing the 800 miles to a distant whaling station in an open boat. The suffering he and his crew experienced are almost unfathomable, but he returned for the remaining crew bivouacked on Elephant Island—and not one member of his crew perished. Principled leaders serve others through their actions, and service to others is a critical test to perform on our preflight checklist when searching for a job that leads to significance.

You don't have to be a leader to serve others, and we can serve others through our jobs in many ways. My wife, Anne, has a primordial fear of bugs. It's irrational. I have heard screams from various rooms in our home that would have guaranteed her a lead role in any of the *Friday the 13th* movies. I've tried to cure her to no avail.

Then she found Sam, the "bug guy." The other day Anne greeted

> *One reason so many people are frustrated with their jobs is that they cannot connect what they are doing to a meaningful or lasting outcome.*

Sam with "You'll never know what a hero you are in my house. I have no bugs." Sam serves us consistently, courteously, and competently, spraying his bug elixirs all around the outside of our home. When he goes to work, he should have no doubt that he serves others in his job.

PREFLIGHT CHECKLIST ITEM 4: PROVIDES MEANING

One reason so many people are frustrated with their jobs is that they cannot connect what they are doing to a meaningful or lasting outcome. For example, in many jobs, workers don't often see how their work impacts the customer—they cannot connect action to accomplishment. They're simply buried in an activity such as filling out forms for a loan application or putting a wheel on a car that they will never see again. In a call center where an employee actually talks to a customer, he's still an anonymous voice trying to engage people who don't really want to be on the phone. It may not feel meaningful. Making sure that a loan is qualified for underwriting and putting a wheel on a car are critically important jobs, but in and of themselves most jobs will prove unfulfilling if they are not viewed as meaningful and connected to a larger purpose.

Meaningful means purposeful, important, substantive, and consequential. Evidence of the need for meaningfulness exists all around us. Biographies, portraits, statues, monuments, tombs, and namesake buildings are everywhere. Even carving our initials into a tree or on the side of a rock is a symbolic gesture that we exist—*I was here, and I matter.* We want to be remembered.

> *All great characters in stories are the ones who give their lives to something bigger than themselves.*
> —DONALD MILLER,
> BLUE LIKE JAZZ, 2003

Our work is one of the biggest ways we're remembered. The expression "pride in my work" means that what I have done is an extension of me that may even remain after I am gone. When we don't perceive that our work is meaningful, we feel diminished. I have a deep yearning to endure, and what I did in life, my work, defines if and how I will be remembered. It's why the psalmist prayed, "Lord, establish the work of my hands."[8] Just look at the obituary page of any newspaper. The headlines almost always describe what kind of work the deceased did, because it captures how we are most likely to remember the person who died.

A prime reason that our work becomes meaningful and endures is because it's "noble." Although not a word that most of us use regularly, aspiring to be noble guides us toward a life of significance. Nobility is characterized by high moral character, courage, generosity, honor, and magnanimity.

Our media-saturated society places a much higher premium on entertainment value. While I enjoy laughing at the neurotic and convoluted sagas during the reruns of *Friends* and *Seinfeld*, I wouldn't describe endlessly drinking coffee and just hanging out as particularly noble. Although these programs entertain us, they don't always provide us with great role models for noble pursuits or meaningful work.

Whatever we're doing with our lives or considering doing, it's good to ask ourselves, does this pursuit really possess the seriousness worthy of our life energies? Ultimately, we want to invest in something meaningful; we want our work to be noble, consequential, generous, honorable, and enduring. At the end of our lives, will we have given ourselves to a calling bigger than self-fulfillment? Will it inspire us to achieve something greater than simply filling up twenty-four hours a day with activity?

Given the investment of time and energy that we all put into work, it seems critical that we start with the premise that our work must be meaningful and purposeful. It certainly includes what we do, but it also involves the perspective we maintain in our work.

Most long for a life of significance and purpose. Given the investment of time and energy that we all put into work, it seems critical that we start with the premise that our work must be meaningful and purposeful. It certainly includes *what* we do, but it also involves the *perspective* we maintain in our work.

Three masons were laying bricks on a construction project still in the early phase, so it was not clear what was being built. A curious passerby asked each of the workers what they were doing. The first said, "I'm laying bricks." The second said, "I'm building a wall." The third said, "I'm erecting a cathedral." The activities of these three workers were identical, but the perspective was quite different. Some of the people with whom I talk are doing meaningful work, but they need to think about their job differently—to shift their perspective. Most real estate developers are noted for creating office towers, shopping centers, or apartment complexes. One well-respected developer points out that he builds communities that help people create deeply satisfying lives. If you cannot see how your work is purposeful, important, substantive, and consequential, you either have the wrong perspective or maybe you have the wrong job.

TWO GUYS AND A DREAM

Early in 2006, in a national news magazine article, Susan Headden writes about education entrepreneurs Mike Feinberg and Dave Levin, who founded "a national network of public schools that has posted stunning achievement gains and shattered all manner of myths about the academic capabilities of minority kids."[9]

Inspired by U2's *Achtung Baby*, Feinberg and Levin created a plan through which students are placed in an environment of rigid discipline, high standards, and hard work. Their *Knowledge Is Power Program* has changed the lives of thousands of inner-city children. After describing the hardships, triumphs, and failures, Levin summarized his work by saying, "We don't go to bed at night wondering why we are on the planet."[10]

Teaching elementary children is clearly not a fit with my abilities and personality, nor may it be with yours, but don't we *all* long to fall in bed at night not wondering why we're on the planet? As the tree of my life adds rings, I stand amazed at how quickly the years pass. With each ring my conviction grows that great fame or wealth, even if I could achieve them, are insufficient reasons to get out of bed in the morning and invest my days. If I cannot give myself to work that enriches the lives of others and endures beyond my own transient enjoyment of the moment, then I will have considered my time on earth wasted.

Engaging in work for which we have passion, that fits with who we are, that serves others, and that is meaningful is neither simple nor easy; however, if we are committed to a life of significance, is there really an alternative?

Note to reader: For an online exercise that encourages you to evaluate your present or a prospective position, using the four dimensions described in this chapter, go to runwiththebulls.net *to access the computer-scored assessment.*

4

GETTING TO THE ARENA

Our destiny is largely in our own hands. If we find,
we shall have to seek. If we succeed, it must be our own
energies and our own exertions. Others may clear the road,
but we must go forward, or be left behind in the race of life.
—FREDERICK DOUGLASS, FORMER AFRICAN-AMERICAN SLAVE
AND ABOLITIONIST LEADER, 1866

A few summers ago, my brother-in-law, Carl, took me and several of our children climbing on the southernmost of a group of volcanic mountains known in Eastern Oregon as the Three Sisters. The snow-capped rim of the South Sister towers majestically above the desert floor. A disciplined planner, veteran outdoorsman, and Eagle Scout, Uncle Carl carefully mapped out our route and inventoried the gear and food needed for our assault of the famous peak weeks in advance. Just before the trip, the boys and I went to the basement to assemble our camping gear. With his prodigious checklists, it occurred to me that Uncle Carl might be overdoing it a bit on the preparation. After all, this was a family outing, not an expedition to the top of Mt. Everest.

Several nights later, I watched a breaking news story about the dramatic rescue attempt of a group climbing Mt. Hood, just north of where we would soon be camping. While trying to lower an extraction stretcher, the evacuation helicopter's rotor blades hit the side of the mountain. The helicopter crashed to the ground, burst into flames, and rolled hundreds of yards down the steep precipice into a pile of twisted metal—the tragic consequence of attempting to rescue some ill-prepared hikers. The newscaster pointed out that every year people die of hypothermia, avalanches, falls, and other mishaps in the Oregon mountains. In this case, the unpredictable and constantly changing conditions of the back country totally outmatched the planning, preparation, and skill of the hikers who died. Carl insisted that we plan and prepare as if our lives and the lives of our children depended on it because they did!

Our plan called for us to leave the trailhead early on the first morning and backpack to a base camp halfway up the mountain. We would then make the final ascent very early on the second morning so that we could get off the top of the mountain before the mid-afternoon thunderstorms turned the summit into no-man's-land.

The varieties of reds, blues, oranges, and pinks against a backdrop of green ponderosa pines, piercing blue sky, and patches of glistening snow near the stream took our minds off anything but the mesmerizing beauty around us.

After several hours of trudging up the trail, our muscles aching under the load of fifty-pound backpacks, we stumbled into the first of hundreds of meadows carpeted with spectacularly beautiful summer wildflowers. The varieties of reds, blues, oranges, and pinks against a backdrop of green ponderosa pines, piercing blue sky, and patches of glistening snow near the stream took our minds off anything but the mesmerizing beauty around us. With the peak of the South Sister looming in the distance, we continued to navigate the well-marked trail. As we labored up the mountain, we could see all three Sisters and our intended base camp nestled in a small meadow a mile-and-a half ahead under the purple shadow of the South Sister.

That night we played around the crater-formed lake and watched a billion blazing stars double their number in the perfectly mirrored reflection of the icy glacial water.

Pots started banging at 4:45 a.m. in the frigid morning air. Our sleepy band stumbled from tents complaining, "It's way too early . . . we just went to bed." Carl briefed us on the challenge before us. We needed to traverse the glacier, but with no sun to warm its icy surface, the glacier would be frozen for hours and difficult to cross. The sun, still below the eastern horizon, threw a few wispy threads of light onto the glistening glacier field that separated us from our goal, and I wondered if that goal was worth the difficulties we might encounter.

Aghhh! Wading barefoot across a stream formed by snowmelt to move some stones forming a path for the group to walk across jolted me awake. The thirty-eight-degree air felt warm to my feet in comparison with the water. Robert Frost's poem, "Fire and Ice," questions whether we would rather freeze to death or burn up. I had always chosen freeze to death, but that stream made me rethink my decision.

After crossing the icy stream, we encountered our first indication of trouble when someone tried to form a toehold in the surface of the glacier. The frozen snow on top of the glacier required three or four firm kicks to establish adequate footing, and the enormity of crossing a mile of glacier suddenly dawned on us. Our troop looked like a flock of Canadian geese, frequently trading the lead while the rest of us followed in the footprints of the climber in front. One of the cousins lamented, "This is impossible . . . we'll never make it across!" The footing would not get easier until about eight o'clock, when the sun's first direct rays softened the surface. Four arduous hours after the difficult trek started, our group spontaneously erupted in jubilation as we finally reached the beginning of a trail leading to the top of the mountain.

Our joy was short-lived, and groans commenced within seconds of starting up the path. No one had anticipated the treacherous footing caused by loose volcanic pebbles. At one point my niece fell to her knees and screamed, "My eyes, my eyes!" Volcanic dust had blown underneath her contact lenses causing excruciating pain. Progress in the thin, windy air above the tree line was grueling, tortuous, and painfully slow. We sweated profusely from climbing but were chilled by the high altitude's cold air. The sun bore down intensely through the thin atmosphere, and our destination still loomed in the distance.

Around noon, our bodies were exhausted—our brains had gone numb hours before. Crossing over a ridge of jagged rocks, we suddenly arrived at a plateau just below the top of the mountain and stumbled across a huge snow field seventy-five yards wide. We started smiling for the first time in seven hours. Before climbing the final thirty yards to the pinnacle, we found a natural shelter from the wind where we gratefully ate lunch.

With our hearts pounding from climbing the final stretch to the summit, it seemed we could see the entire western United States in the panorama. Even though the wind kept us bent over, everyone jumped and shouted with excitement at having made it to the top. The clear desert air made huge distances seem close. To the north in Washington State, Mt. Saint Helens with its cone-shaped top reminded us that we were standing on top of an active volcano that could erupt again in our lifetime. The joy of this experience so overwhelmed us that no one thought about the pain we had just experienced.

We forgot about our exhaustion when we discovered that we could hurry down the mountain with ease by sliding on the same volcanic pebbles that made going up so difficult. When we reached the glacier, our weary band became even more reenergized as we ran and skied on our feet down the entire glacial expanse. What had taken us four hours to climb, we slid down in twenty minutes! Gravity was finally working for us. I don't think the winner of the World Series that year was more celebratory than our group as we whooped and hollered our way down the glacier.

PREPARING AS IF OUR LIVES DEPENDED ON IT

In stark contrast to the doomed nautical fiasco described in the previous chapter, our mountain climbing expedition was *intentional*. We encountered major obstacles and unexpected challenges, but thanks to Carl, our careful planning undergirded our ability to improvise and change course as needed. We celebrated the accomplishment in one case, while we brooded for days over

> *While not all intentional people are successful, all successful individuals are intentional.*

the harrowing consequences of the other. The clarity of purpose, intentionality, and forethought of our mountain expedition led to a very different outcome.

These two stories provide important contrasts with respect to *how* we reach our "arena"—our life destination. When we choose the more difficult commitment required to achieve a life of significance, it simply does not occur by chance. It requires intentionality.

While not all intentional people are successful, all successful individuals are intentional. Intentionality precedes any major accomplishment. There are four primary elements found in the attribute of intentionality

—a strategic mind-set, disciplined preparation, going on the offense, and courage in the face of difficulty.

A STRATEGIC MIND-SET

Strategic thinkers constantly reflect on how to achieve their purpose and goals. They contemplate, research, plan, rehearse, and get others involved in helping them accomplish whatever they set out to do. They are deliberate and premeditated in their actions—they possess a *strategic mind-set*.

Strategists view work and life like a chess game. They're always thinking several moves out. How could a particular person, resource, or event help them in their quest? They become resourceful and find creative ways to overcome obstacles that block their progress.

Strategic thinkers are constantly gathering new information to inform their decisions and remain flexible to avoid getting painted into a corner—they keep their future options open. Being opportunistic and receptive to new information is a hallmark of good strategists. It's not unusual for opportunities better than the original plan to come along; therefore, we need to be alert, flexible, and responsive.

Intentionality also prompts the discerning strategic thinker to say no to other opportunities, even when they are attractive—in order to stay the course. In his best-selling book, *Good to Great*, Jim Collins described the "Hedgehog Principle," which says we must know when to say no to a good opportunity that distracts us from our primary mission. Collins points out, "Hedgehogs see what is essential, and ignore the rest."[1]

We've all experienced the "ready, fire, aim" approach with the predictable results. Living and working intentionally means that we are thoughtful and strategic in our efforts. We take aim at a clear purpose and actively take steps to reach that purpose.

Much has been written on the importance of saying no, and I tried to get the leaders of a client organization to read a few of those books. Their failing company, which attempted to invent a new loading machine for freight cars, just couldn't seem to stay the course. The leaders were so open-minded, you thought their brains were going to fall out. Even though they had created a sound product, they were too undisciplined and opportunistic to stay with it. Every new idea that came along—on an almost daily basis—became the company's new strategic focus. A lot of investors lost money because the company wouldn't stay focused on its core competency and make *it* work. Many individuals have approached their careers with the same lack of focus, bouncing from one "opportunity" to another with no master plan to guide their decisions.

DISCIPLINED PREPARATION

Being intentional requires that we must prepare by gathering the information and resources needed to successfully reach our intended destination. Uncle Carl knew some of what to expect on our expedition, but some aspects were unpredictable. We had to prepare for both. We checked the weather before we left, but we were prepared for any changes in the forecast. Our group was thankful that we had all brought ponchos when an unexpected deluge occurred on the second day. Many hikers succumb to hypothermia in fifty-degree temperatures. They're just not ready for how quickly body temperature can drop during a chilly rain shower.

Just as we tried to understand the conditions that could impact our expedition, it is vital to learn about the external forces that affect our careers. Many of the young professionals I know subscribe to unrealistic expectations about what is required to reach senior level positions in their companies. They often are not clear about the training and experience needed to function effectively in the executive suite. They are unaware of the unwritten rules and informal practices that exist under the surface of almost every organization.

> *Disciplined preparation involves intense personal scrutiny, including looking at ourselves to determine how our personal characteristics may help or hinder the achievement of our goals.*

Disciplined preparation involves intense personal scrutiny, including *looking at ourselves to determine how our personal characteristics may help or hinder the achievement of our goals.* Executives who fail to achieve their potential often lack self-awareness. These corporate underachievers fail to take advantage of their strengths and are more susceptible to their weaknesses. In many cases an executive overuses a strength, and then his personal asset becomes a liability. Over 2,500 years ago, a famous Chinese general, Sun Tzu, wrote, "If you know the enemy and know yourself, you need not fear the result of a hundred battles."[2]

"JUST DO IT!"

Nike built its brand around the marketing phrase, "Just Do It." In coining this powerful and memorable phrase, Nike surfaced the problem that so many of us experience—getting started. That first step is often the hardest. Rock climbers sometimes use an expression, "make the

move." During an assent of a rock wall, climbers must release a perfectly good handhold or foothold to make progress up the face of the
rock. The gnarliest moves require the climber to let go of his hold and
lunge for the next hand or foothold. Just before making a move, a
climber can freeze. In reaching for the next handhold, the climber
risks injury or even death should the next handhold not work.
Experienced climbers know that they must reach a commit point and
then make the move. Not enough forethought makes the move too
risky. Too much analysis, called a *vapor lock*, paralyzes the climber.
When a vapor-locked climber finally gets around to making the next
move, it's often tentative and even more dangerous.

We typically don't enjoy getting outside our comfort zone, especially
when the stakes are high. Contemplating a move makes us anxious, but a
willingness to *just do it* separates those who thrive in the world of work
from those who struggle. A mid-level manager who worked in a client
organization for over twenty years before his company downsized him
called me right after the layoff. David had wanted to start his own business for many years, and this seemed like the perfect time. Knowledgeable
experts he consulted about the commercial viability of the product he
intended to manufacture indicated he had everything he needed to be
successful in a new venture, and he even had a few customers ready to
commit. As I listened to him deliberate about the pros and cons, he
reminded me of the TV detective, Monk, trying to straighten out every
detail in his world. David's obsessive-compulsive decision making style
caused him to vapor lock on a decision to launch the new business. The
viability of actually starting the new business diminished with the passing
of time, and he ended up taking a job very similar to his previous position in another large company. His dream will die in obscurity—a great
venture intended to serve many that never left the starting gates.

Louis L'Amour, who wrote over 200 western novels, often leads his
heroic characters into a dead-end canyon with outlaws guarding the

entrance. The guy in the white hat concludes that the only way out is to plan a daring escape. In the middle of a moonless night, the hero and his compatriots quietly saddle their horses and take off riding through the middle of the outlaw camp, six-shooters blazing. The clear principle of L'Amour's stories is that in life you're almost always better off making a move—going on the offense rather than simply staying on the defense.

Making the move for many of us can be as simple as posting for a new job, getting our résumé in the right hands, or taking that person to lunch to network about a new position. Crossing the commit point requires courage and decisiveness, but a life of significance requires that we make a move.

Many people stay passively holed up in their circumstances, knowing that their job, living situation, or group of friends is a dead-end canyon. Making a move with our careers is almost always the best approach. Doing excellent work in our jobs, no matter what our position, is critical, but it may not always get us noticed. Successful individuals volunteer for additional assignments. They offer to prepare the presentation and even to make the presentation. When they have down time, they offer to step in and help others. They communicate their aspirations to important members of the organization. They post for jobs with more opportunity or new skills to acquire.

At some point, every successful person has made a move. Bill Gates dropped out of college and set up a business in his garage. A client organization's first products were manufactured at the family's kitchen table. Many organizations start up in similar ways. Making the move for many of us can be as simple as posting for a new job, getting our résumé in the right hands, or taking that person to lunch to network about a new position. Crossing the commit point requires courage and decisiveness, but a life of significance requires that we make a move.

Mary, the head of a large department of a highly successful company, entered the organization at age twenty-two as an administrative assistant. At age thirty-seven she served as a vice president and member of the company's senior management committee. How did she accomplish this meteoric rise in fifteen years?

There were a number of obstacles. There were no women in management in her company and no indication that women would ever be welcomed into the inner circle. In a company where everyone with a significant position had an undergraduate degree and often an MBA, she hadn't finished college.

Although a bit reticent at first, Mary consulted with her manager, and it became apparent that her lack of a degree would interfere with her desire for more responsibility and challenge. Her life circumstances (needing to work full-time and expecting her first child) made getting the degree a daunting challenge. There was zero certainty that getting her degree would result in her advancement in the company.

After contemplating her decision for several weeks, this young administrator just did it—she took the first step and enrolled in college at night. Over time she took other bold initiatives, such as volunteering for projects to grow her knowledge and skills. Many times she sought out someone in the organization to learn what she could about his role. When consultants worked in her department, she asked questions to get an outside perspective. She maintained others' confidences, so they trusted her with sensitive information. She sought out opportunities to be mentored by senior members of management, which eventually included the president of the company. She joined professional organizations and completed their certifications. She learned from her setbacks. Mary reached out to individuals who were not necessarily supporters to understand whatever reservations they had about her actions. She was highly intentional, so there was very little wasted motion in her efforts—every step served the organization but also moved her forward in skill and knowledge.

You might be thinking that Mary was unique. Actually, just about every senior executive in any organization could tell a similar story of focused effort, skill development, getting wise counsel from others, and taking the initiative to gain more responsibility. It all started with her decision to make that first move—to finish college despite the obstacles.

COURAGE

When we realized how difficult it would be to traverse the glacier, it was very tempting to declare premature victory, take a few pictures at the base of the glacier, and return to our base camp. In some cases, perhaps we are a little too easily thwarted, so what helps us to persevere? The promise of what we would experience at the top of the mountain gave us the conviction and courage to persevere.

One of my favorite movies is *Indiana Jones and the Last Crusade.* In the climactic scene the bad guy (Walter Donovan), Indiana Jones, and Indy's father all converge in a cave thought to house the Holy Grail, which they believe has healing powers and will give eternal life to the one who drinks from it. Several enemy soldiers have already died attempting to cross the lethal gauntlet between them and the Grail. In desperation, the bad guy shoots Indy's father, knowing that only water from the Grail can heal him. Jones must find a way through the gauntlet to save his father. With a sneer of contempt, the villain shouts at Jones, "Now is the time to decide what you really believe!" Does Indy *believe* the Grail is real? Is he willing to risk his life to pursue his quest in earnest?

Don't miss the "belief" part. Many people I meet suffer from "about-ism." They talk "about" what they want to do, such as going back to school or about posting for a new position or about trying to find a job for which they have passion. I always sense an underlying equivoca-tion. These are ideas, possibilities, or dreams, but they're not *beliefs* undergirded with conviction for which the person is willing to take significant risks.

Few of us would say that we are courageous. Courageous acts are not performed by people with a personality trait called *courage*. Courageous acts are performed by normal people who passionately believe in what they are trying to do—the urge to act on their conviction becomes compelling. Everyone who has ever performed a courageous act was afraid. Their conviction about what they believed simply outmatched their fear. A courageous person does not talk "about" an idea, but rather acts on what he or she really believes.

Inevitably when we attempt something significant, challenges of many different types usually follow. Detractors often speak up and question the wisdom of our decisions. After graduating from college, my son, Jim, worked for four years in the US Congress and found his work to be very challenging and significant. He also knew that he wanted to accomplish more in his career, so after months of deliberation, he concluded that he wanted to go to business school to further develop his leadership skills. To his surprise, an important mentor challenged his plans: "Jim, why do you want to leave a perfectly good job? You have a stable position with a good salary, excellent benefits, and you work with many interesting people." His mentor's questioning of his plans jolted Jim, but he concluded that he must press forward.

> *Courageous acts are performed by normal people who passionately believe in what they are trying to do— the urge to act on their conviction becomes compelling.*

It is totally normal to struggle with how to move forward in our lives. Often the forces in opposition seem insurmountable. How do we cross the glaciers in our lives when returning to base camp is what we really want to do? Where do we get the discipline to persist and the courage to stay the course? It rests in what we really believe.

Quoted at the beginning of this chapter, Frederick Douglass (1817–1895) was truly one of the most remarkable figures of the nineteenth century. Born into slavery in Tuckahoe, Maryland, Douglass overcame the ravages of slavery to become the first African-American formally presented to a US president and assigned a senior governmental post. It doesn't take much imagination to grasp the effects of slavery on a person's self-esteem and motivation. In spite of his circumstances, Douglass believed that he must do something significant with his life. With help from his former owner's wife, he taught himself to read and write so that he could study the Bible and become educated. He later escaped to Massachusetts and gained his personal freedom. He then pursued a lifelong mission of helping others through his work as a minister, a statesman, and an eloquent speaker for the abolitionist movement. His accomplishments, his influence, and his international recognition cannot be overstated.

Douglass's bedrock faith was interwoven with a unique sense of personal responsibility to act . . . to go on the offense. He believed unrelentingly that his life had a purpose and that he would not become a victim of his life's circumstances. Douglass epitomized a life of significance, intentionality, action, and courage—simple but not easy.

Summary of Section 1

THOUGHTFUL COMMITMENT

Our commitments, whether carefully chosen or not, exert great power over our lives. They energize us and guide us with focus and intentionality. Thoughtful commitment leads us to pursue a sincere and steadfast purpose with our lives and our work, and it transforms our existence from mundane to extraordinary.

To run with the bulls without getting trampled, run with thoughtful commitment!

AUTHENTIC CHARACTER

5

RUN BY THE RULES

This above all: to thine own self be true, and it must follow as
the night the day, thou can'st not then be false to any man.
—WILLIAM SHAKESPEARE, *HAMLET* (ACT I, SCENE 3)

Eerie blue light illuminates their pensive faces. Sweat and streaks of black grease glisten on their tense, furrowed brows. Dread-filled eyes dart furtively to their captain, desperately hoping he is right to make this dive. Panicked, hushed voices now whisper, "She's turning around." The pinging of the enemy's sonar increases as rapidly as their heartbeats. "Keep it quiet, boys." The cramped gray compartment filled with pipes and gauges packs the crew too close together. Noxious odors from the diesel fuel and sulfuric acid in the sub's batteries make the air almost unbreathable. The flickering lights threaten to plunge them into darkness. "Deeper, chief, it's only pressure." One man's quiet sobbing and the awful creaking of twisting metal portends the deadly implosion each man knows to be seconds away. Suddenly, the deafening blast of depth charges rocks the boat violently—fire, smoke, screaming—and then the dreaded leaks spring from weakened seams in the hull. Broken bolts fire with the velocity of bullets. At first a trickle, and then an explosion of freezing water—the hull is breached.

To evade an enemy, a German submarine *(Das Boot)* descends far below its safe depth, and the captain pushes the boat and its crew far beyond their psychological limits. Under excessive depth pressure, the integrity of the hull is compromised.

Many of the great war movies are about submarines—*The Hunt for Red October, Crimson Tide, U-571,* and one of my favorites, *Das Boot.* Naval officers often refer to the "integrity of the hull" because nothing is more important than the trustworthiness of the hull of a submarine. A compromised hull puts the boat in jeopardy. A trustworthy hull enables the submarine to do its work—to go underwater and complete its mission.

Most dictionaries define *integrity* as honesty and reliability, and both of these qualities are foundational to effective organizational life. The psalmist captures this idea when he prays, "May integrity and upright-ness protect me."[1] Our integrity or trustworthiness protects us just as the hull of a ship protects the sailors inside. Our integrity enables us to do our work effectively. Any thoughtful person will ask, "Is my personal hull trustworthy, reliable, and structurally sound?"

Our humanity makes us terribly fragile, and we're particularly vul-nerable in those areas that truly distinguish us, such as integrity. Com-promised integrity impairs our performance and our ability to work.

WHAT'S IN YOUR WALLET?

News of Houston-based Enron Energy Corporation's scandal domi-nated headlines for months in 2004, and former Enron Chairman Kenneth Lay went on trial in early 2006. On May 25, 2006, Lay was convicted on six counts of conspiracy, securities and wire fraud, and four additional charges in a related trial. Quite unexpectedly, Ken Lay died of a heart attack on the morning of July 5, 2006, while vacationing in Aspen, Colorado.[2] Lay's colleague and Enron's chief executive, Jeffrey Skilling, was convicted on nineteen of twenty-eight counts.[3] Enron's employees lost over 2,000,000,000 dollars from their pension funds and over five thousand lost their jobs due to Enron's collapse.[4] Ironically, Enron's published values statement prominently featured *integrity* as a core corporate value.

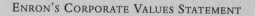

ENRON'S CORPORATE VALUES STATEMENT

Respect: We treat others as we would like to be treated ourselves. We do not tolerate abusive or disrespectful treatment. Ruthlessness, callousness, and arrogance don't belong here.

Integrity: We work with customers and prospects openly, honestly, and sincerely. When we say we will do something, we will do it; when we say we cannot or will not do something, then we won't do it.

Communication: We have an obligation to communicate. Here, we take the time to talk with one another . . . and to listen. We believe that information is meant to move and that information moves people.

Excellence: We are satisfied with nothing less than the very best in everything we do. We will continue to raise the bar for everyone. The great fun here will be for all of us to discover just how good we can really be.[5]

Many companies spell out their corporate values. It would be hard to imagine a CEO or senior leadership team that did not aspire to conduct their business with integrity. Would we even consider working for an organization that didn't aspire to honesty and reliability? You may have one of those laminated cards in your wallet or on your desk with the mission statement and the values of your organization. In one impressive display, a company I visited had their values artistically etched into beautiful tinted glass walls in the entryway.

The challenge is that sometimes organizations transact their business dealings in a manner inconsistent with their expressed code of values. It's always a bit shocking when the media brings to our attention an instance in which corporate executives compromised their integrity. I would have been floored if someone had told me years ago that the accounting firm of Arthur Andersen would one day go down in flames. For eighty-eight years, Andersen was the standard-bearer of accounting firms and an assumed paragon of corporate integrity, but the venerable old firm sank after the Enron scandal, among others. What took many decades to establish disappeared in a few months.

Through a unanimous ruling, the US Supreme Court actually cleared Andersen of any wrongdoing in the Enron scandal on a technicality, but the news came so long after the fact that the company had already been decimated.[6] Even the appearance of impropriety can bring down a giant. Insiders also confirmed that Enron did not bring down Andersen. It was actually an endemic pattern of ethical compromises in accounting practices and conflicts of interest in a number of client organizations that undid the firm.[7]

A lack of integrity seriously compromises any effort. Submarines are designed to go to great depths in the ocean and withstand tremendous pressure, but underwater, any weakness in the hull puts the whole boat at risk. An incomplete weld or a weak seam can be the source of the initial leak, but inevitably that weakness creates others. Rarely do individuals make one big compromise of their integrity. One's compromise of character and integrity most often occurs in a series of tiny steps (a white lie, a rationalization, or looking the other way). Tiny leads to small, small leads to larger, and larger leads to . . . Soon big issues don't appear so big any more. Author Derek Kidner sums it up well when he observes, "We deceive ourselves by the smallness of our surrenders."[8]

HAZARDS TO THE HULL

There are many possible challenges to the hull of our integrity. The following are a few of the most important in the work setting.

TESTING THE LIMITS

When William and I ran with the bulls, there were only two rules. First, don't touch the bulls. This rule ensured that the animals would be treated with respect. As importantly, touching the bulls endangers the runner, since the disoriented animals are already pretty ticked off. Some runners got away with grabbing a horn or running along with their hand on the bull's side. Others weren't so lucky—they ended up gored and trampled. As I mentioned earlier, the second rule was, "Once down, stay down until the bulls pass by."

We all know people who push ethical limits. When I speak to corporate groups, I often ask how many members of my audience have personally witnessed unethical behavior at work. The response is rarely below 100 percent. Staying just inside the edge of what is right is a certain recipe for compromise.

Hank Greenberg, CEO of the global insurance conglomerate AIG, was noted for testing the limits and ultimately failed the test. A 2005 *Fortune* article documents how Greenberg "got away with it (the frequent crossing of legal and ethical lines) because he produced spectacular results."[9] Greenberg masterfully manipulated ambiguities in the law and complexities of the business, saying, "All I want in life is an unfair advantage." AIG's independent board members finally decided that Greenberg was over the ethical edge and asked for his resignation on May 13, 2005, amidst a series of ongoing investigations.

THE GREAT EFFECT OF SMALL CAUSES

A minute bubble led to great drama in the nearly catastrophic flight of United Air flight 232 from Denver to Chicago on July 19, 1989. The fan disk in the DC-10's rear engine exploded, severing all three hydraulic lines despite the low odds of this event ever happening—a billion-to-one chance. An investigation later discovered that a titanium ingot used to manufacture the fan disk had a tiny imperfection that finally weakened to the breaking point. It took eighteen years and 15,503 takeoffs and landings to discover the problem. A jumbo jet with no hydraulics at 37,000 feet promised a spectacular death for the more than three hundred people aboard, all because of a microscopically small bubble of nitrogen not completely dissolved in the titanium ingot. The bubble was the tiny cause of a huge effect. Only the extraordinary skill of the crew provided a safe landing for the aircraft.

Flaws in integrity are like that little nitrogen bubble. They may not show up for a long time, but the pressures of business over time find that point of imperfection. Anyone who has worked for a public company understands the pressure of Wall Street's expectations for quarterly earnings—these pressures are real, and they typically roll down through many layers in an organization. I've experienced them. A company I worked for missed analysts' expectations by two cents a share one quarter, and our stock value dropped 20 percent in a day. Everyone who owned shares inside the company as well as the outside stockholders took a huge hit. An intact hull of integrity is critical to withstand this type of pressure.

Common rationalizations for unethical behavior are "No one will ever know," "This won't affect anyone else," or "I built this place from scratch—I deserve to get more for all I've done." The act itself may seem small, but the implications for the organization are big. A small decision can foster huge effects, though it sometimes takes a while for that nitrogen bubble to wreak havoc.

While our jobs may not put us in position to cook the books and defraud shareholders of billions of dollars, we're just as vulnerable to rationalizing unethical actions. Retail businesses estimate that at least 5 percent of gross income is lost due to dishonest acts of employees. Restaurants, for example, are especially vulnerable to employee theft of cash and food, even giving free food to friends. Many organizations are vulnerable to the theft of time—how many employees put in the full day for which they were paid?

HOW MANY CHICKENS

A chicken farmer carried some of his chickens to market in his half-ton pickup. The cages were stacked high above the cab and hung out far beyond the bed walls. As he drove down the highway, every few seconds he slapped a short section of two by four lumber against the outside door panel. The loud sound startled the chickens, and many of them fluttered to the tops of their cages. When someone finally asked the farmer what he was doing, he explained, "I got one ton of chickens on a half-ton truck, so I gotta keep half of them in the air all the time."

Regardless of our position in an organization, we have significant ethical responsibilities—how we handle expense accounts, use of a company car, use of the Internet, or how we use sick leave, just to name a few.

Being thoughtful and self-governing in these areas grows our capacity so that we keep up with the ethical demands tied to increasing job responsibilities. We must make sure that our ethical capacity keeps up with our growing responsibilities so that we don't load a ton of ethical challenges on a half-ton truck.

Many enter the workforce with the highest ethical aspirations. Most experienced executives say that in the last decade or so, there has been a dramatic increase in competitive pressures and an escalation in customer expectations. CEOs feel a constant pressure to meet quarterly earnings forecasts. These and many other pressures wear people down over time. Without a firm footing of conviction based upon absolutes, alternatives are considered. A compromise never entertained in theory suddenly becomes thinkable in practice . . . and then doable.

Many movies draw attention to the subject of integrity, but one of the best ever in a business genre was the 1987 Oliver Stone classic, *Wall Street*. Michael Douglas plays the character Gordon Gecko, who insidiously corrupts a young stockbroker named Bud Fox, played by Charlie Sheen. Gecko knows that he wants Fox to work for him, but he shrewdly challenges the foundations of his integrity by suggesting that his traditional values are outdated: money is what's really important. Over a period of time, Gecko relentlessly breaks down the naïve broker's resistance. In a particularly memorable scene, Gecko paints an alluring picture of what wealth can do for Fox:

> And I'm not talking about some $400,000-a-year working Wall Street stiff flying first class and being comfortable. I'm talking about liquid. Rich enough to have your own jet. Rich enough not to waste time. Fifty, a hundred million dollars, buddy. A player . . . or nothing.[10]

Although Fox knows that the action Gecko asks him to take is illegal, with no hull of integrity to protect him, he can't handle the pressure. Fox finally implodes and says, "Alright Mr. Gecko, you got me."

WHAT IS INTEGRITY . . . REALLY?

We've all heard a lot of graduation speeches or messages from our CEOs stressing the importance of integrity, but it's easy to be confused about right and wrong. Contributing to this confusion is the fact that so many traditional beliefs have been challenged in the news media, television, film, philosophy, and the courts of public opinion.

Integrity is ultimately a bit abstract—it's sometimes hard to know what we *should do* in a given work situation. For example, how do you view the following situations?

INTEGRITY SCENARIOS

Clearly Wrong	Probably Wrong	Gray	Probably Right	Clearly Right
1	2	3	4	5

_____ Take an extra thirty minutes at lunch to get a haircut.

_____ Use sick leave to go to a ball game.

_____ Tell your manager you have finished a project even though you haven't.

_____ Use a company credit card for personal expenses in a pinch (to be paid back later).

_____ Shop on the Internet during work time.

_____ Flatter a coworker insincerely because you need her help on an assignment.

_____ Report that a team member is finished with a project when actually it's not quite ready.

_____ Accept gifts from an outside vendor.

_____ Call in sick when you're just having a bad day.

_____ Don't lie about the status of a project, but hold back some key facts from your manager about its readiness.

What guides us to the right conclusions in situations like these and others that we encounter every day at work? While we may not know whether an action is right or wrong in every instance, it's always better for us to choose the harder right instead of the easier wrong. Why? Because our integrity protects us and guards our reputation—why ever put our personal "hull" at risk?

Many moral/ethical questions are black and white, such as stealing property that belongs to our employer, but many other issues that we face in the workplace seem gray, including some of the circumstances listed in the integrity scenarios. Sometimes the notion of integrity is abstract, and it's not clear what we are to do. Ideally, we need guidance that is more concrete and practical.

> *It's always better for us to choose the harder right instead of the easier wrong.*

Trustworthiness is the quality that's really at the heart of integrity. *Integrity* is the external label for the internal trait of trustworthiness. If we act in a trustworthy manner, we are more likely to make solid choices in integrity-challenging situations.

TRUSTWORTHINESS—THE ROI FACTOR

Trustworthy means *worthy of trust*. Whose trust? In the workplace we are trusted with the assets of those for whom we ultimately work—the stockholders or owners. Our trustworthiness also impacts our coworkers who depend upon us to complete our part of any work assignment. When we work for an organization, we are caretakers or stewards of the owner's assets. This includes the company's money, its facilities, its customers, its reputation in the community, the quality of its products or services, its market positioning, and the well-being of its employees.

Ideally, we preserve the value of those assets, and we skillfully manage our part of the assets so that owners actually make money on their investment. Not only do our knowledge, skill, and effort play a huge role in the creation of financial value, but also our trustworthiness creates ROI—return on investment.

Trustworthiness is like the oil between the moving parts of a machine. Not long ago, I interviewed a senior executive from a Fortune 100 company and asked him, "What is the most important factor in achieving your organization's business results this year?" I fully expected him to point out their new strategy to aggressively pursue a segment of the retail market. His surprising answer was "trust." When I asked him to elaborate, he explained that no strategy would work if people in his company didn't trust each other. He further stated that it was the individual and the collective *trustworthiness* of his team that would determine the business results.

Trustworthiness makes a person distinctively valuable to the organization. When I analyzed what made the difference between executives who were successful and those who derailed, one key differentiator was their personal trustworthiness—how they handled their time, effort, initiative, and creativity.

We must also pay attention to the little compromises. Even a tiny irregularity opens the door for bigger problems—just remember the nitrogen bubble. It's why some companies fire someone for a $25.00 "compromise" on their expense reimbursement form. It may be a small amount of money, but it indicates a lot about the person's character.

With the notion of *trustworthiness* in mind, you might want to go back to the integrity scenarios on page seventy-five to see if you have additional clarity. Do any of your choices change as you think about being a steward of your organization's assets?

THE BALANCE IN OUR TRUSTWORTHINESS ACCOUNT

Trustworthiness is like a bank account—we can make deposits and withdrawals, and there's always a balance. We know people at work who have a healthy balance in their trustworthiness account, and we also know people who are overdrawn. It's terrible to not be trusted. When someone's trustworthiness account is overdrawn, others do not rely on that individual. They even avoid the untrustworthy person and certainly don't share important information with him. The untrustworthy person is quietly ostracized. His opinions are discounted and his credibility constantly challenged. Coworkers marginalize the untrustworthy person at every turn. While there are many ways of making deposits and withdrawals from our trustworthiness account, two are especially critical—truthfulness and reliability.

TRUTHFULNESS

Truthfulness reflects our willingness and ability to be open, candid, sincere, and forthright. It manifests itself in two ways—with ourselves and with others. Truthfulness with others is rooted in candor with ourselves—intrapersonal honesty. Shakespeare's dictum, "To thine own self be true," reminds us how inextricably linked these two are.

> *Truthfulness reflects our willingness and ability to be open, candid, sincere, and forthright.*

Be Truthful with Ourselves

It's sometimes very hard to be honest with ourselves, but self-honesty is the cornerstone of trustworthiness. We can be quite skillful at hiding our true motives from ourselves and developing false but justifiable reasons for what we really want. Our insecurities drive us to subtle forms of self-deception; for example, just think of *rationalize* as "rational lies." Similarly, it's easy for us to mistake sincerity for truth. Just because someone sincerely believes something doesn't make it true. We know people who have been sincerely wrong.

The most effective leaders I know possess great self-awareness. They're always carrying on an honest inner dialogue about their actions and their motives. This type of honesty allows them to get beyond selfishness and ask what is best for those around them. The leaders I've seen who really examine themselves often believe in a higher set of standards outside themselves. They possess a *magnetic north*—a set of objective principles that they follow to guide them to their decisions.

One executive I consulted with asked himself challenging questions whenever he made important decisions. He fostered an inner dialogue to ensure that his actions passed the test of ethical scrutiny. He

> *The linchpin of trustworthiness— always tell the truth.*

also invited others to challenge the trustworthiness of his decisions. Using others as a sounding board has great merit, particularly when decisions possess moral ambiguity.

Try the "News Test." When you're not certain about what to do, consider if you would want to explain your actions to an investigative reporter from the *New York Times*. A variation is the "Parent News Test." Would you want your parents trying to explain what you did on *60 Minutes*?

BE TRUTHFUL WITH OTHERS

Human behavior is complicated, especially when it involves another human. We spend eight to twelve hours or more at work every day, and in that time most of us interact with dozens of people. Our trustworthiness account balance grows or diminishes through how we treat others in the workplace. We foster trustworthiness in our relationships with others at work when we communicate honestly.

The linchpin of trustworthiness—always tell the truth. Whether with a coworker, your team, or the whole organization, be honest. Dishonesty is a seedbed for cynicism and mistrust. You can overdraw your trustworthiness account in a hurry with a lie.

The February 21, 2006, issue of *USA Today* ran a story with the headline "RadioShack CEO quits over items on résumé." David Edmondson resigned from his CEO post after the board pushed him out over issues of credibility. He claimed on his résumé to have graduated from college, when he had not. College records showed that he had completed only two semesters of coursework. Board chairman Leonard Roberts pointed out that the public's trust is dependent upon the corporation's integrity and trust.[11]

> *A liar is not believed even when he tells the truth.*
> —CICERO, DE DIVINATIONE
> (ACT II, SCENE 7)

One of my clients gives its job candidates an "honesty test" by asking a very simple question: "What was your college grade point average?" Most people don't remember their GPA down to the hundredth of a point, but they do know the range. After the interview, someone at the company contacts the registrar of the candidate's college. It is not uncommon to find individuals who overstate their GPA. If a person is not going to tell the truth about something as simple as a grade point average, why should the individual be trusted on matters of substance that could affect the success of the organization?

RELIABILITY

Late in the game when the score is tied, a major league baseball manager usually goes to a favorite pinch hitter whom he can count on to get a clutch hit to get on base or drive in a run. When a job has to be done right, corporate managers usually go to the same people for help—they're the ones with a positive balance in their trustworthiness account because they're dependable, consistent, and steadfast. Reliability is the second major way to make deposits in your trustworthiness account. Three actions especially define how we act with reliability in the workplace.

KEEP YOUR COMMITMENTS

To raise the balance in our trustworthiness account, we must *do what we say we're going to do*. For some of us a deadline is a date to have a project completed. For others, it's a time to start getting serious about it. Being trustworthy means we do what we agreed to do and when we've agreed to do it. Being trustworthy also means giving fair warning if a commitment cannot be kept due to factors outside our control. In these rare circumstances, we should go to all those affected and discuss the implications. The reasons for any change in the original agreement need to be true and compelling—not an adult version of "the dog ate my homework." We can reforge the agreement with others in an overt, respectful, and responsible manner.

In many organizational settings, we use the word *commitment* to describe something we've agreed to do. Try substituting the word *promise*. It changes the tone and the level of obligation and seriousness that we feel. A promise seems more binding.

PURSUE EXCELLENCE RELENTLESSLY

We must not only do what we say we will, but also do it with excellence. To increase your account balance, complete your assignments with a higher level of quality than expected. If your manager asks you to make a recommendation on a new long-distance provider, go the extra mile. Develop the criteria a provider must meet to satisfy your organization's needs. Summarize how the various vendors compare against the criteria. Display your findings on a color-coded graph so that the findings of your research make decision making easier. Prepare your recommendation with a clear rationale. Anticipate the types of questions that your manager will ask and focus the discussion on the points you know to be of greatest interest to the decision maker.

We must not only do what we say we will, but also do it with excellence.

Excellence requires that we constantly refine and improve our skills. It could be as simple as taking a computer class or as involved as graduate school. Airline pilots constantly train in simulators to develop their skills and to practice their procedures in a safe context. They can then handle real emergencies with confidence. Many professional groups, such as lawyers, doctors, teachers, accountants, and psychologists have continuing education requirements to be sure that members of the profession remain competent in their work. Regardless of what we do, we must continue to learn and grow our skills to perform our jobs with confidence and effectiveness.

RUN BY THE RULES

Rosie Ruiz won the eighty-fourth women's Boston Marathon on April 21, 1980, with a record time of 2:31:56. The Cuban-American runner had qualified for the 26.2 mile Boston race by running in the New York Marathon six months earlier. Race photographs in Boston show the strain and exhaustion on Ruiz's face as she struggles to cross the finish line at the end of the grueling endeavor.

One big problem. Suspicious race officials eventually determined that she hadn't actually run the marathon. She started the race and then apparently just hopped the subway and ran the last mile or so to cross the finish line. Experts speculate that Ruiz didn't intend to win the race, but she unintentionally stepped back into the race too early, several minutes ahead of the next female runner. Although Ruiz insisted that she completed the race, organizers concluded that the overwhelming evidence proved that she hadn't. Race officials disqualified Rosie's win.[12]

Earlier in this book, I suggested that a race works well as a metaphor for our work lives, and I indicated that we should run to win; however, in order for the race to have meaning, it must have rules. Rosie cheated. She crossed the finish line first, but her win was meaningless because she didn't compete according to the rules of the race.

There are rules in the race of life. Rights and wrongs do exist. In the postmodern world, many believe that moral standards are relative, usually relegated to categories like *appropriate* and *inappropriate*. In a favorite *New Yorker* cartoon, the prophet Moses comes down the mountain to remind his followers that there are some absolutes.

"Well, actually, they <u>are</u> written in stone."

Establishing our personal trustworthiness at work is especially challenging when it seems like many in the workplace follow a different set of rules. In most organizations employees strive to be upwardly mobile; it's an accepted norm that we grow in our careers by seeking more responsibility or control—the more people or the bigger budget we manage, the better. We all know the person who is constantly angling for his own advancement. His or her focus is not on doing the job but on getting a bigger title and more money and status in the organization. Direct reports and peers can't stand the individual, and his or her staff often feels devalued and ignored. This person will do just about anything and say just about anything to get ahead, and, sadly, sometimes this tack works.

It's confusing. Being rewarded with a promotion is normal and expected for effective performance in our jobs. Using manipulation, deceit, and gamesmanship is quite another matter—yet it seems to work sometimes. So why should we try to follow the rules? Because trustworthiness protects us like the hull of a submarine. It was at the core of what made many of the people I interviewed over the last twenty years successful in their careers. People's misdeeds eventually catch up with them—just look at some of the examples earlier in the chapter.

Ultimately, it gets back to honesty with ourselves. In the complicated maze of our motives and desires, we can sometimes manage to convince ourselves that our behavior is OK, even when our conscience denies us peace. That lack of peace should always be a valuable signal warning us that our intended actions may not be right.

I have no illusions about what I've written in this chapter—it's neither simple nor easy, but it is essential. The pressures of work and life always challenge a life of significance. Trustworthiness requires constant vigilance and uncompromising self-honesty to keep our "hulls" intact.

6

KEEP ON RUNNING

Never, never, never . . . give in.
—SIR WINSTON CHURCHILL, ADDRESS AT
HARROW SCHOOL, OCTOBER 29, 1941

The river just seemed different. My sons and I had fished the Deschutes many times and knew the spot well. It's considered one of the premier fly-fishing streams in North America and is known for its fierce steelhead—a type of freshwater trout that hangs out in the ocean for a few years with the big fish and then swims back up the mountain streams to spawn . . . with an attitude.

William and I pulled on our chest-high waders and rigged up our fly rods, discussing whether to fish downstream or up. The stream appeared sullen. Usually a peaceful, easygoing stream, today the blue-green water was a cloudy brownish gray. Our normal crossing spot was too deep, so we stayed on the side with the boulders. The surrounding forest looked foreboding, and the occasional deer were nowhere to be seen.

William caught a small rainbow trout on a wet fly and then quickly released it back into the frigid water. Upstream from where we stood, the boulder field stretched a hundred yards across. In chest waders it was a major effort to climb across the big rocks to the trail along the river, so I said, "William, let's go through the forest so we don't have to climb the boulders." He wanted to fish that spot for a few more minutes, so we agreed to meet upstream. I climbed the steep bank to the trail through the gigantic ponderosa pines with their resin-oozing, yellowish-brown bark. I slogged along in my water-logged wading boots until I turned off the trail and reached the bottom of the bank now upstream from the boulder field. Looking downstream, I noticed that William was no longer fishing there. After about ten minutes, I started to wonder what was taking him so long to join me, and after another ten minutes, I decided to go back and find out.

Near our original spot, I slid down the bank and looked upstream and downstream—no sign of him. Curiosity quickly became concern. I stumbled along the trail, calling out for him in the dense forest where my loudest whistles and calls fell instantly flat. Concern grew into apprehension, which quickly morphed into panic.

People who experience panic attacks hover along a thin line between levelheadedness and irrationality. I was there, and I knew it. My mind was not working . . . I couldn't make a decision. I couldn't organize my thoughts and calm down enough to focus, plan, or even pray.

Panic became terror. What could have happened? Could he have slipped, hit his head on the big rocks, and fallen into the rushing stream unconscious? How could I drive back and tell Anne that I had lost our son? My voice took on a new sense of desperation. I ran back again to where I had left him. Catastrophic thinking took over as I retraced the same trail a third time, and the minutes became quarter hours.

Racing aimlessly up an unfamiliar trail, the forest began to close in on me. My hoarse voice seemed to die in the darkness a foot from my face. Even in the cool, dry air, streams of sweat stung my eyes.

Suddenly, I stumbled into a small clearing, and there scratched in the red dirt was a message, "Dad—this way." The arrow made of small limbs pointed to the northeast. At first my muddled brain could barely make sense of the message, and then I knelt and ran my finger around the letters . . . tears of relief. At that point I didn't even need to see William—his words *were* him, and they were enough.

Ten minutes later I found him. He couldn't get the words out fast enough. "Dad, I'm sorry. I took a wrong turn and totally lost my bearings." The Oregon forest is so dense and enormous that it's easy to understand how people get disoriented and lost. Every effort to find the right trail simply put him farther off track. We chided each other for violating our buddy rule and made an ironclad, lifetime pact to never, *ever* get separated in the wilderness again.

Many people I meet in the workplace have lost their way. Some are captive in high-paying but boring, purposeless jobs; they're paid to be miserable. Others are anxious and stressed about their work, the huge changes in their organizations, or the potential consequences of being out of a job. Sometimes I even see panic and despair in their faces. We don't think clearly when we're under excessive stress, and our productivity slides; it's a vicious circle. It would also be so much easier if leaders just communicated: "Everything's ok, we're going to get through this; here is our direction." But very often leaders seem lost themselves and fail to communicate.

THE MISERY INDEX IS UP

Earlier in this book, I pointed out that as many as 85 percent of Americans are unhappy in their jobs. The workplace is filled with misery and distress. Incompetent managers lack even basic interpersonal skills and clumsily try to lead their unwilling associates. Scott Adams became famous writing about these managers in *Dilbert*. Adams frequently points out that people e-mail him about actual events in their organizations, providing him with material for the cartoon strip. I received an e-mail recently that said, "When trouble arises and things look bad, there is always one individual who perceives a solution and is willing to take command. Very often, that individual is crazy."

There are notable exceptions. Some organizations' cultures are healthy, supportive, and uplifting, but many modern organizations' cultures are toxic. Some companies foster a dog-eat-dog competitiveness even among their own employees.

The social contract between many companies and their employees has changed irrevocably in recent decades. Delta Air Lines once displayed an undying commitment to its employees, and for many years had a no-layoffs policy. Sometimes pilots had to unload bags, but they had jobs during the lean times. The employees reciprocated with a fierce loyalty to the company. During a recession, the employees of Delta all pitched in and bought the company a new jet—a gleaming symbol of their love and appreciation for the company. As I write this chapter, Delta just entered bankruptcy. While certain external forces played a big part (globalization, competition from low-cost start-ups, the rising price of oil), much of the blame can be laid at the feet of a group of leaders who took huge pensions and left the company in dire straits. They put their own interests ahead of the well-being of the company and the other employees. Shock waves went through the Delta community when details of these secret pensions were leaked to the press and employees realized they had been betrayed. The contract of trust was broken—perhaps forever. Delta's oldest retirees may eventually lose their pensions because of the bankruptcy. Many young families have taken multiple pay cuts, and the future of their jobs is always uncertain. Current employees vacillate between cynicism and anxiety.

Although change and tumult have always been a normal part of the workplace, there seems to be more disorder and danger than ever. We long for control and predictability, for our worlds to make sense or to at least seem somewhat rational. We have colleagues who make good decisions, and the business does well. We then see the same coworkers let go or moved to an irrelevant position and watch them be replaced with incompetent people. It just doesn't make sense.

FLYING THROUGH IT

Those who are successful handle uncertainty and turbulence in some unique ways. The following identify some of their most effective approaches.

HIGH PERFORMERS GAIN ALTITUDE TO MAINTAIN PERSPECTIVE

During my son Jim's first year of college football, he played on his school's junior varsity team. Parents and friends were invited to stand on the sideline just behind the coaches, so we took advantage of the opportunity to see his games up close. Football at eye level is absolute chaos. The hitting, the cracking of helmet against helmet, the yelling, the swearing and hurling of insults, the sweat pouring off the players' faces, and the coaches' attempts to provide direction created mayhem. We were so close to the action that it made no sense, and it was almost impossible to follow the game.

The next season we sat up in the stadium, well above the field. It was a totally different game because we could look down on the field and see the plays unfold. It was more obvious why the quarterback substituted a new play at the line of scrimmage in response to an unexpected defensive alignment. It's very understandable why coaches on the field use their headsets to talk to their assistants in the skybox: they have perspective and can see opportunities and dangers not visible when too close to the action. The connection with the skybox helps the coach devise plays he might not ordinarily think about.

When I observe successful people, I see that they have the ability to gain altitude in order to get perspective. They emotionally detach themselves from their immediate context to get a higher view. They get off the field and into the skybox. The workplace is often fraught with emotion. Sometimes our interests get pitted against others' interests when there are limited resources. Perspective gives us a better view of the whole game and takes the focus off what is happening directly in front of us. Perspective helps us invent new solutions not normally recognizable under stress.

I once worked with a senior executive whose favorite question when faced with a problem was, "What's the worst thing that could happen?" The answers typically varied. Certain scenarios might be bad, like missing the market analysts' projections and seeing the stock drop, but usually the worst consequence was *not* catastrophic. His response was always the same. "If that's the worst thing that can happen, then we can survive that. Let's start looking for solutions." This wise leader maintained a good perspective that prevented catastrophic thinking on the part of his team.

The right questions facilitate skybox thinking. It may even help to "diagram" the problem if you're more visual. To get perspective, ask these types of questions:

- What is the *real* problem?
- How does the problem impact me?
- Who else is involved with the problem, and how does it impact them?
- What does each party gain if the problem is positively resolved for everyone involved?
- What is the right thing to do?
- Is there a better way or better time to implement the solution that benefits all involved?
- Is anyone acting disingenuously or lacking integrity?
- How would a wise but uninvolved person view the problem?
- What risks must I take to propose a more encompassing solution to the problem?
- Are the potential benefits of the solution worth the risks?

HIGH PERFORMERS SEE OPPORTUNITIES OTHERS DO NOT

Fly-fishing experts recommend carrying a pair of polarized glasses. The special lenses cut the sun's glare and allow the fisherman to see into the water to locate fish. If he is wading upstream, there could be fish right in front of his feet that he can't see because of the glare on the water. Without the glasses, a fisherman can walk too close to the fish and scare them—a missed opportunity. The polarized lens allows the fisherman to look past the glare into the water to then drift a fly near the fish.

In the workplace, problems often have an emotional glare that prevents us from seeing solutions and opportunities right in front of us. High performers can see through the glare and find answers that others cannot see.

When I work with teams, I often ask a question if I feel their discussion is not generating insightful solutions. I usually concoct a scenario in which the team buys the company and gains a controlling interest. I then ask them to identify the changes they would make in short-range, mid-range, and long-range time frames. Often the discussion becomes very energetic and the answers carry more impact and creativity. The participants generate inventive ideas such as acquiring the competitor to build market share. Of course, my follow-up observation is, "If these are the solutions you would implement as an owner acting in the best interests of the business, why wouldn't you recommend those ideas in your present role?"

The purpose of the exercise is for the participants to put on "owner glasses" rather than looking through the usual lenses that may prevent them from seeing new opportunities and new solutions. How would they run the business if they had to filter opportunities and risks through the lens of their own financial stake? This is actually a good exercise for all of us to look more carefully for solutions we might not otherwise see.

To help remove the glare from a problem in your organization, ask:

- What factors are obscuring the right answer to the problem?
- In what way could my biases be obscuring the right answer?
- Could the best solution impact me negatively or make my job irrelevant?
- How do I feel about that?
- If we viewed this as an opportunity instead of a problem, what would be different?
- If this was my company and a solution put my own money at risk, what would I do?
- What could we change immediately, in six months, in a year?

HIGH PERFORMERS SEE THE WORLD IN MORE COMPLEX TERMS

Have you ever looked at a *Magic Eye* drawing? It is usually a page with a wash of color but no clearly recognizable image. Yet if we allow our eyes to go unfocused while staring at the page, suddenly a three-dimensional image appears. It is a remarkable optical effect.

A critical element in surviving today's organizational turbulence is to look for three-dimensional, more complex solutions. Anyone can be a master of the obvious and see two-dimensional solutions. What's more difficult is to find solutions that rise above the ordinary. Typically a two-dimensional solution pits one person or department's position against another's. Different parties blaming one another is a dead give-away that a two-dimensional solution is in play. A garden variety law-suit is an example.

We see warring factions in the workplace on a daily basis. One organization's sales force frequently requested that members of the service arm of the company be present during sales calls to answer technical questions. The service providers complained that many of the sales leads were poorly qualified, so their time spent on the sales calls was wasted and took them away from serving existing clients. Over time, the service providers became much less available and declined to participate in sales calls. In retaliation, the sales team went to senior management to complain that their results were poor because the service providers were never available to help pursue new prospects. Management urged patience and collaboration on both sides to no avail. Collaboration actually declined, and ill will grew.

A manager named Brook finally suggested that a team of sales and service providers meet regularly to review the prospect list. She focused the team on common goals: "We need new clients and new projects

Too often, members of the organization become indignant about problems that are fundamentally rooted in differences in perspective rather than true moral breaches.

in our existing clients to reach our mutual goals. We also have to make sure that we're using our service providers in the most effective way."

Agreements were forged to insure that sales and service concurred on the strategic value of joint participation on sales calls for every prospect. The discussions were spirited, but both sales and service committed to reach agreement on how to best use the company's resources. The meetings became much more productive and collaboration increased dramatically. The service providers began to steer the sales staff toward new leads. When both sides acknowledged the complexity of each other's needs, a mutually beneficial solution emerged.

We often see a limited, two-dimensional view in the workplace when parties with conflicting interests look for a solution that responds to only their part of a problem. We have a natural tendency to pick sides and see relationships in black-and-white terms. When someone crosses you, it's normal to think of all the reasons why you are right and he is wrong. Some issues in organizations do rise to the level of right and wrong when there are moral/ethical issues that deserve to be confronted, like the corporate scandals we looked at earlier; however, too often, members of the organization become indignant about problems that are fundamentally rooted in differences in perspective rather than true moral breaches.

Knowing that problems are more complex than a first glance reveals, high performers look for higher-order principles that guide their decision making. For example, asking the question, "What is in the best interest of the stockholders, customers, and employees?" often provides clarity in decision making.

People don't act according to the truth but rather to the truth as they perceive it.

High performers value well-managed conflict because it sharpens discussion and generates solutions from higher-order principles. They also recognize that *how* we solve the problem is frequently as important as *what* the solution is. If a problem is solved effectively, our team collaboration improves.

Successful executives know that human perception is complicated. Depending on our unique perceptions, we can see a problem very differently, and the truth is often in the middle of those perceptions. Savvy individuals recognize that even when someone's perceptions are inaccurate, those ideas are still the basis for their decisions. People don't act according to the truth but rather to the truth as they perceive it. To argue with someone's perception can be like spitting into the wind. Teams are often better off trying to shift the focus to a mutual goal rather than trying to establish the correctness of a given team member's perception.

Dealing effectively with complexity always involves asking good questions:

- Who else is impacted by any solution I devise?
- Have I involved others in the discussion of the problem and possible solutions?
- Am I at risk for "trampling on sacred burial grounds" in trying to solve this problem?
- Are we really solving the problem or just dealing with a symptom of the problem?
- Is there someone with "institutional memory" who could give more understanding of the problem?
- Sometimes solutions created in the past to solve problems made perfect sense at the time, but conditions have changed. Why was the existing solution put in place?
- Why is an existing solution no longer a good one?
- Are we at risk for "changing for change's sake?"

HIGH PERFORMERS GROW THROUGH ADVERSITY

Over the years I have frequently asked successful executives about what most contributed to their effectiveness in leadership. Without exception, effective leaders report that they grew through facing challenges, solving difficult problems, correcting mistakes, and enduring hardship.

One brilliant leader with whom I worked had a favorite saying, "Everybody ought to get fired once." He had been fired from a job earlier in his career and went without work for a number of months. During that time he came to grips with who he was: an arrogant, dictatorial, detail-obsessed micromanager for whom people hated to work—and he deserved to be fired. When he finally landed his next position, he was a changed man. Still brilliant but now humble and gracious, he focused on helping others to be successful. The hardship refined him and made him a servant leader.

Some of my most enjoyable and challenging consulting assignments over the years have been with family-owned companies. Frequently I've been asked to help identify and develop talent in a succeeding generation of the family. I often discover that the founders and even the second-generation leaders are smart, resourceful, mentally and emotionally tough, and great at generating customer loyalty. They learned their business from the ground up. The children of these business builders sometimes grow up in families with more money and greater advantages. Their summers are spent at the lake or traveling.

When the children or grandchildren of the founder eventually enter the business, their position in the company does not rest on their work experience or upon the accomplishment of difficult goals. Their position was attained solely by virtue of membership in the family. As a parent I understand how we want our children to have more than we did, but I also have observed the pitfalls.

What is missing here? The first generations didn't get tough and savvy by going on vacation. They grew strong through working and solving the normal problems that occur in any small business—for example, mowing neighbors' lawns. They learned that if you didn't take care of your lawn mower, it would let you down at key times. In the businesses they eventually started, the machines became bigger and more complicated, but they knew the value of preventive maintenance through the hard lessons of their youth.

One of my favorite movies of the '90s was *Tommy Boy*. After Tommy's father dies of a heart attack, it is apparent to everyone in the company except Tommy, played by Chris Farley, that he is completely

Character and emotional toughness are not built through ease but through the hardship that life deals very freely.

incapable of running the manufacturing company his father started. To save the company from bankruptcy, Tommy and the company's financial manager, played by David Spade, go on a road trip to sell their products to distributors. At first their sales efforts are a disaster. Then the adversity they experience begins to benefit Tommy as he discovers more about himself and learns how important the business is to the workers in his hometown. Character and emotional toughness are not built through ease but through the hardship that life deals very freely. We become mentally and emotionally stronger through challenges, difficulties, and adversity.

A REAL-LIFE ROCKY GOT UP

No one ever thought the fictional Rocky could get up after his brutal opponents pummeled him to the mat, but he did. John Keeble was a real life Rocky. He founded the Financial Service Corporation, one of the most successful financial services firms in a highly competitive securities industry. As much as any CEO I know of, John persevered in adversity and remained a vibrant, values-driven leader. Quite open about his failures in business and the resulting personal hardships, John left FSC twice under pressure from the board. In his absence the company floundered, and in both cases he returned to restore the reputation of the firm as one of the leading broker dealers for independent financial planners. Eventually an insurance conglomerate acquired FSC. Keeble later started another firm, which was acquired by a different insurance powerhouse a few years later. In both acquisitions, stockholders scored major returns on their investments.

Over the ten years I had the privilege of consulting with John and his two firms, he grew remarkably as a leader and as a person. Although highly educated at Vanderbilt University and Vanderbilt Law School, he had no formal training in business leadership. He was a voracious reader and a student of management, reading the *Wall Street Journal* cover to cover every day without exception.

It is impossible to overstate the emotional impact of twice being fired from the company he helped found. Lesser individuals would have faded into obscurity. John exemplified a blend of personal humility and fierce resolve to build a company undergirded by exemplary values. After he returned to run FSC, John decided to be a different and more skillful leader. He guided the company through a dramatic period of growth. He not only recruited new representatives to join the firm but also acquired a number of smaller firms.

Through the adversity of his early career and even later betrayals, John always rose from the mat a wiser person. He became less naïve about people and their motives. He became more pragmatic and able to solve complex problems involving many competing interests. While remaining a gentleman, he became tougher and able to say no to unreasonable demands. Through all the hardship he never lost his integrity, his love of people, his sense of humor, his faith, or his vision.

He worked tirelessly on being a better communicator, drawing wisdom from a group of trusted advisors with whom he held court on a frequent basis. John's most trusted advisor was always his savvy and insightful wife, Dottie, who inevitably helped him gain the perspective he needed when solving complex problems. He never forgot his humble personal origins, nor did he become arrogant or vindictive against those who had earlier ousted him from the company.

John's most noteworthy ability was hiring other strong people. His legendary gift for recruiting brought together some of the most talented players in this industry. His skill at enlisting others was rooted in the vision and values he held so strongly.

John continued to grow personally and professionally until he succumbed to cancer, which he fought courageously for many years. He crossed the finish line with an unfinished "to do" list of articles he intended to write and wisdom he intended to acquire.

I visited John at his home a few months before he died. In a large stack lay the articles he planned to read that day. In another stack were proofs from several articles he had just written for leading journals.

Many recognize John as the "grandfather of the financial planning industry" and credit him for the simple but profound concept of "spending less than you earn and investing the difference." Countless individuals have retired with financial security because of his wide-ranging influence. I believe John's amazing personal and professional accomplishments are in direct proportion to the hardships he overcame. His personal resilience and wisdom grew directly out of his willingness to learn from and grow through adversity.

Perhaps your life circumstances are hard right now. When you are unhappy at work, it inevitably colors how you feel about life. In our jobs, it's not unusual to feel that we

> *Although instant gratification certainly has its rewards, most good things in life require persistence.*

are under someone's thumb or that the value of our personal stock is low. You may feel like you're lost in the deep woods of your job, never to return.

It is very easy for us to develop resentment for our bosses. A boss may be incompetent, unfair, insensitive, rude, uncaring, and possess a whole host of other undesirable characteristics. Perspective plays a critical role. It's often helpful to remind ourselves that "this is not the end of the story." Change occurs quickly, so the people and the circumstances may be very different sooner than we expect.

Although instant gratification certainly has its rewards, most good things in life require persistence. For example, there is a strong correlation between income and education. The problem is that school is often boring and learning new information can be tedious. Persistence requires that we have a long planning horizon. For example, if a person wants to be a physician, the real winnowing out occurs during the fall semester of his or her freshman year in college. That's when the tough decisions get made—*do I study organic chemistry tonight, or do I go out?* It's when a lot of first-semester biology majors pursue a new interest. While the preparation to become a physician may be an extreme example, most significant accomplishments in life are preceded by delayed gratification—setting aside what you want to do for what you need to do in order to reach your goal.

We typically picture Winston Churchill with deep creases in his petulant face, reflecting the hardships he knew as a child and as an adult. The famous line quoted at the beginning of this chapter ("Never, never, never . . . give in") powerfully electrified the assembled students at Harrow. The power of the words rested in the character of the speaker and in his relentless, enduring pursuit of life significance.

It is impossible for me or anyone else to fully understand whatever adversity you may be facing. I can say with confidence that most highly successful people who found significance in life and in their work faced huge difficulties and challenges along the way. Although the path forward for you may be neither simple nor easy, I encourage you in the strongest terms: don't give in!

7

DON'T GET DISQUALIFIED
FROM THE RACE

Good judgment comes from experience . . .
and a lot of that comes from bad judgment.
—COWBOY WISDOM

It was a glorious Sunday afternoon in the foothills of north Georgia. My sons and I were enjoying one of our favorite Sunday after-lunch activities. We drove to a little-known spot near our home with a view to the Appalachian Mountains that we called the Overlook. When visibility was good, you could see forever.

The fall air was pleasant, and the sun-filled sky was so bright and clear you had to squint to look at it. You could see the mountains to the north, the lower plains to the south, and the Chattahoochee River meandering around the sprawl of Atlanta in between. The sun cast a glow on the city below, and the yellows, reds, and oranges of the fall foliage were spectacularly beautiful. It was one of those days that just made you feel happy. No one in our family was thinking about the mortgage payment or Jim's math test or the long trip I had to take the next morning. For those few tranquil minutes, I began to think world peace really was possible.

A few minutes after we arrived, a couple drove up in their new red pickup truck to enjoy the view. Riding in the truck bed was a vintage black lab that jumped out and introduced himself—his name was Jasper. He was one of those affectionate, never-met-a-stranger types of dog. Jasper also knew what kind of day it was, and he was going to suck out all the marrow of life that beautiful afternoon.

Without warning, the exuberant Jasper took flight over the four-and-a-half-foot guard wall snaking along the edge of a deep precipice. We all watched with horror as Jasper plunged 120 feet to the bottom of the cliff below. Although it happened with lightning speed, everything moved in slow motion. I honestly couldn't tell whether the scream I heard came from me or from Jasper's traumatized owners. I instinctively pulled the boys close. The man yelled and cursed as they jumped into their truck and tore down the twisting road to where Jasper lay below. The smell of the burning rubber from his screeching tires fouled the air as their sound became indistinguishable from the woman's hysterical sobbing.

In an absolute state of shock, the boys and I stood motionless for several minutes, holding each other. We walked over to our car and drove down the mountain. Stopping to see if we could help as we approached the red truck, we peered over another wall thirty feet above where Jasper lay on the ground between his two owners. The man looked up and slowly, sadly shook his head. Jasper was dead.

After returning home everyone slipped off quietly for the rest of the afternoon. How could a day of such indescribable beauty be marred by such a sad occurrence? As I wrestled with my own confusion, I knew I had to help the boys find some kind of meaning and put this dark event in perspective.

As Anne and I talked about what had happened, my grandmother came to mind. She was full of wisdom and wit and had a way of distilling complex circumstances into simple principles. I knew immediately what she would have said. Not one to have been politically correct about animal rights, or anything else for that matter, Grandma Goldie would have said, "That dog should have looked before he leapt." While her answer wouldn't have shown deep empathy for Jasper's grieving owners, she would have reached the root of the problem. Jasper was reckless and undisciplined. My grandmother's imagined wisdom turned this sad experience into a life lesson for my young sons.

We all know people who act just like Jasper. They have boundless energy, but it's undirected and impulsive. We often see a lack of self-management in our colleagues at work, precipitously jumping over the walls of good judgment. Perhaps we've even jumped over them ourselves a time or two. How many times have we regretted saying or doing something? With respect to character, we have talked about integrity and persistence. In this chapter, there are additional failures of character which can knock us out of the race.

LEAPING BEFORE YOU LOOK

Some executives are particularly bad about not looking before they leap. Within a few months of taking over an established manufacturing conglomerate in the textile industry, a brand new CEO impulsively restructured his company in an attempt to align the business units more effectively. Many observers immediately knew the restructuring wouldn't work mainly because of those whom the CEO put in charge of the manufacturing plants: many were simply not respected by the employees who actually made the company's products. Within hours of his announcement, people at all levels of the organization began to update their résumés. One of the new manufacturing plant heads—noted for his brashness, duplicity, arrogance, and constant schmoozing with senior management to promote his own personal advancement—bludgeoned his employees with interpersonal clumsiness, poor communication, and ineffective handling of the organization's changes. Knowledgeable insiders gave it six months before the best players would leave his part of the organization. At last count, most members of a very stellar team were either gone or would be soon.

It is not unusual for organizations to create and to periodically review a list of high-potential employees. These "high pos" have greater-than-average potential to rise in the organization and make a significantly larger contribution. It is particularly interesting to study those who were thought to have great potential but failed to live up to it because of a weakness.

OFF THE TRACKS: COMMON DERAILERS

Individuals who derail are usually blinded by their own lack of awareness; they miss the connection between their behavior and its impact on others. They have impenetrable blind spots. The prison warden in the movie *Shawshank Redemption* lacks basic common sense in dealing with the prisoners, so Tim Robbins' character asks him, "How can you be so obtuse?" The warden's arrogance, greed, and narcissism eventually lead to his downfall. Although any number of factors can cause someone to derail, the following are particularly significant.

POOR INTERPERSONAL RELATIONSHIPS

Whether with direct reports, peers, managers, or even customers, poor working relationships are often cited as a primary reason for derailment. Many managers advance because of their technical skills, even when they have a major interpersonal deficit. They depend on their technical abilities and fail to develop the skills essential for managing others. Under stress they become more critical and demanding. Their interpersonal deficit makes an even greater impact as these individuals move higher in the organization.

Whether a leader or an individual contributor, these individuals don't make good team members. They're often out of touch with the needs of others and have trouble working collaboratively. They don't trust the members of their staff, and no one likes to work for them.

One senior executive with whom I consulted grew his technology business rapidly and profitably. As skilled as he was in the technical aspects of his job, he failed to get others to work together, because he tended not to collaborate with anyone himself. He didn't listen and could take the wind out of the sails of a meeting faster than anyone I had ever seen by attacking the participants and their ideas. He appeared to build himself up by diminishing others.

Other confident and capable members of the organization wouldn't tolerate his abusive management style, so he had trouble retaining strong talent. I cringed whenever he visited the field offices, because I knew the company would lose some great people once they saw him in action. An acquiring company eventually eliminated his position and basically wanted nothing further to do with him—he had burned too many relational bridges along the way.

ARROGANCE: A TERMINAL CASE OF CERTAINTY

Arrogance is often identified as one of the leading contributors to executive failure. These individuals overestimate their own capabilities. You even may have wanted, at some point, to say to your boss, "You're not always right." Arrogant individuals have tremendous trouble adopting the new frameworks and behaviors necessary in rapidly changing business conditions. They don't adapt well to changes they haven't authored because they cannot condescend to support a position created by others. Their egos constantly get in the way of their flexibility and their objectivity.

In *Good to Great*, Collins proposed that one of the most distinctive traits of high-performing leaders was humility. These highly effective people were described as modest and calm, yet determined. They rely on inspiring standards rather than personal magnetism to motivate others. They recognize the accomplishments of others and yet hold themselves accountable for poor results. Arrogant leaders are quite different.

> *Arrogance is often identified as one of the leading contributors to executive failure.*

On September 19, 2005, Tyco executives Dennis Kozlowski and Mark Swartz were sentenced to twenty-five years in prison for stealing as much as $600 million from the company. In describing Kozlowski, Assistant District Attorney Owen Heimer said, "He stole. He committed fraud. He committed perjury. He engaged in a shocking spree of self-indulgence."[1] His last comment referred to his wife's $2 million Roman-toga birthday party on the Mediterranean island of Sardinia, which Kozlowski paid for largely with company funds. Kozlowski's arrogance led to an attitude of entitlement: Tyco existed to serve him and his needs. As he used company money to buy a $6,000 shower curtain, he apparently never considered the stockholders and employees of Tyco.[2]

VOLATILITY

These derailers are the Bobby Knights of the corporate world. They may not be throwing chairs on the basketball floor, but their lack of emotional control shows up in numerous ways. They are often moody and hard to please, and their excessive emotionality and hair-trigger tempers make coworkers steer clear of them. No one likes to work for this kind of manager, especially when he's the focus of the volatility.

Volatile managers sometimes play a psychological game called "uproar": they get their way by keeping everyone off balance. After getting their way they immediately calm down, so people working for this type of manager do anything to keep their boss from losing it. Employees learn where the emotional landmines are and avoid bringing up those subjects, even when the work suffers as a result.

A wholesale apparel company I consulted with had an incentive compensation system that was absolutely maddening. Everyone but the chief financial officer thought the system was totally dysfunctional. The CFO had created the system earlier in her career when the company was much smaller. Since then the company had evolved into a complex organization with multiple lines of business in a number of different countries. Different entities now endured vicious fights over who owned and serviced each account. The arguments rarely addressed the customers' best interests; rather, billing credit was the issue because it determined their financial targets.

The real problem was the CFO's volatility. The compensation system was one of her emotional trip wires. Despite overwhelming evidence that the existing system made collaboration totally impossible, she repeatedly told the warring parties to "work it out." Anyone who dared raise the issue felt her immediate wrath. Her irrational emotionality on this subject (and numerous others) created a dysfunctional system and cost the organization dearly in lost productivity and clients.

ALOOFNESS

One of the most frequent executive failures is the tendency to be aloof and uncommunicative. People who act this way are usually critical and demanding. Their aloofness is rooted in an introspective style that makes them detached, insensitive, and dismissive of others.

Shortly after Roberto Goizueta died, the board of the Coca-Cola Company appointed M. Douglas Ivester as chairman and CEO of the huge soft drink conglomerate. He was a logical choice for the role:

formerly chief financial officer of Coke, Ivester had assisted Goizueta in creating Coca-Cola Enterprises (CCE), a separate company created to consolidate many privately owned local bottlers of Coke products. Their success put Coca-Cola in control of the manufacturing and distribution sides of the business. Wall Street loved the approach, and CCE's stock quickly rose in value.[3]

Our jobs are about achieving results that are important to the organizations that employ us.

Although brilliant, Ivester was reported to be awkward, detached, and coldly logical. Because he was so strong in the financial and accounting functions, his strengths as CFO became weaknesses as a CEO. Coke suffered a huge firestorm when Coca-Cola products in Belgium were found to be contaminated. Ivester and his team handled the PR nightmare with frustrating slowness, and stock values quickly eroded under their tentative approach. At first, Ivester alleged that the hundreds of reported illnesses were "psychosomatic reactions." Later, Coke initiated the biggest product recall in its 113-year history. The board soon replaced Ivester with a new CEO.[4]

The *Wall Street Journal* described Ivester as having a "tin ear."[5] He didn't pick up on subtle messages from the people around him and was insensitive to nuances. While arrogance was undoubtedly a factor, the general clumsiness Ivester displayed in addressing the crisis reflected an overall leadership deficit—aloofness and an inability to read other people and situations. This resulted in slowness to act and a disastrous error in public relations.

FAILURE TO ACHIEVE RESULTS

While thought to have great promise at driving the organization to new levels of productivity, workers who derail often prove incompetent in actually achieving results. High achievers do whatever it takes to get results and often show great resourcefulness. In contrast, those who derail don't make sound decisions and fail to take the necessary actions to create strategic alignment with other groups. They don't follow through on actions they've agreed to take and communicate poorly what others must do to achieve good outcomes. Their failure to build and motivate a team around common goals inevitably leads to poor performance.

Ultimately, our jobs are about achieving results that are important to the organizations that employ us. One way of being wise at work is to find out what our bosses value. Metrics have become a consuming focus of the modern organization. It is wise to know what standards our boss views as important and make sure our energies at work are directed at achieving those metric goals. Of course the ultimate benchmark is profitability. One wise executive used to tell me that a primary goal of his company was to make money every month because that contributed to longevity!

INABILITY TO CHANGE

As members of an organization move to higher levels or different departments or organizations, their skills must change. They must be flexible enough to learn new approaches that match the needs of the new situation. Leaders who derail often fail to adapt. When they enter a new department or a new organization, they rely too heavily on methods or models they have used in the past. Unfortunately, these tried and true methods don't always translate.

A seasoned executive took over a business unit that made highly customized refrigeration components for pharmaceutical laboratories. The subsidiary he had managed previously made standard refrigerators for the consumer market, so operational efficiency and consistency were essential. The executive's previous organization tended to employ workers who needed more supervision and tighter methods of control to deliver a consistent product for its customers. The subsidiary he took over required tremendous flexibility to innovate, and its customers demanded highly customized solutions—a very different business model. The employees in the pharmaceutical lab division were highly educated and very "self-managed." They prided themselves in their ability to develop solutions unique to their sophisticated clients' needs.

Leaders who derail often fail to adapt. When they enter a new department or a new organization, they rely too heavily on methods or models they have used in the past. Unfortunately, these tried and true methods don't always translate.

Within months of taking over the custom refrigeration unit, the executive began to make changes. The existing structure fostered flexibility, collaboration, and innovation; the unit was highly profitable, and retention and morale were high. To everyone's surprise, this obtuse executive publicly stated that he preferred the business model he had used in his previous organization. He intended to employ the same high-control, tightly managed system in his new assignment. Morale immediately plummeted. When knowledgeable leaders in the pharmaceutical lab group challenged the wisdom of the changes he planned to make, they were fired. One senior insider told me that if a person set out to intentionally destroy the organization, he could not have done it more skillfully than this individual. The most talented members of the organization left in droves.

In Chapter One, I described a young man in the bull run who violated one of the two cardinal rules: "once down, stay down." The classic definition of a fool is someone who keeps making the same mistake, expecting a different outcome. This young man fit the definition perfectly, at least three times. The derailers described in this chapter also fit the description. They make the same mistakes again and again and are oblivious to the predictable consequences. Eventually their obtuseness derails their careers. My Grandma Goldie, who did not tolerate fools lightly, used to say, "A fool isn't worthless . . . he can at least be used as a bad example." The derailers described here are great "bad examples."

Ultimately, these derailers are failures of character, to which we are all vulnerable. It's critical that we regularly look ourselves in the mirror and ask the tough questions. Am I particularly susceptible to any of these major derailment factors? Under what conditions are these characteristics most likely to surface? How can I manage these vulnerabilities more effectively?

Getting advice from a trusted advisor provides insight and helps us change. Just looking at a few of the "bad examples" mentioned here should compel us to pay careful attention, lest we get disqualified from the race. Derailers often jump over the wall of good judgment because they have not developed some of the seven *Critical Success Factors* to be discussed in the next section. Although simple on the surface, these CSFs are anything but easy.

Note to reader: These derailment factors are included in the online self-assessment located at **runwiththebulls.net**

Summary of Section 2

AUTHENTIC CHARACTER

Our character ultimately defines who we are, and in the preceding three chapters we explored the broad composition of character, including integrity and persistence, along with the factors that cause us to derail in our careers. Our character wraps around us, protecting us like the hull of a submarine—but compromises in our hull can be exposed by routine pressures of the workplace. Compromises take the form of dishonesty with self and others but are also found in arrogance, volatility, and poor interpersonal relationships. An authentic character makes us worthy of trust.

To run with the bulls without getting trampled, run with authentic character!

EXCEPTIONAL COMPETENCE

8

MAKE SURE
YOU'RE FIT TO RUN

I think the guys who are really controlling
their emotions . . . are going to win.
—TIGER WOODS, PGA CHAMPION GOLFER,
IN A 2001 INTERVIEW

A few years ago, a group invited me to speak to their annual leadership conference in Europe, and they included my family on the trip. A month or so before our departure, Anne told me about a lifelong dream to visit Portugal and wondered if we could stop in Lisbon on the way to the meeting. Our travel agent told her that our airfare would change only slightly, so I said somewhat distractedly, "Fine with me." Anne agreed to make the hotel arrangements, and I moved the departure date up on my calendar.

The hotel confirmation arrived a few days before we left, and I went into shock when I saw the exorbitant charge. I asked Anne with visible irritation, "How can we do this? There is no way we can afford to stay in that hotel." Anne calmly explained that she was upset, too, but it was the only hotel that had space available. Then she shared her plan to save money by taking our food with us. She had brought down an old blue suitcase from the attic and filled it with food for our three days in Portugal. At that point it was too late to change our flights without a significant penalty, so we moved ahead with her plan.

After flying all night, we checked into the beautiful Hotel Estoril del Sol and ate our first breakfast from the food Anne had packed. I opened a miniature box of cereal and squirted it with room temperature milk from a carton. My father always described his two grandsons as "appetites with skin stretched over them," and you could tell from their faces that the Blue Suitcase Plan was not going to work well. The view of the Atlantic Ocean was beautiful, but the breakfast was dreadful. Anne noted our grumpy moods and suggested we change clothes and begin our tour of Lisbon.

On the way down, our elevator stopped on the mezzanine level. As the doors parted, we looked straight into the hotel dining room. It looked like a spectacular movie set. With a backdrop of the bluest ocean I'd ever seen, linen-draped tables were laden with magnificent food. Large ice swans and flowers decorated the tables as pleasant waiters attentively bustled around. What I noticed most, however, was how happy everyone in the dining room seemed to be. I knew the reason they were happy—they were eating breakfast in that beautiful dining room.

Sensing trouble, Anne pulled my arm and led us down the stairs out into the bright Portuguese sunshine. After several hours of sightseeing, we stopped for lunch in a park with a shady bench overlooking the magnificent bay. Anne handed me a can of tuna fish with a pull-top ring and some saltines—our lunch. I felt grateful for Anne's resourcefulness, but these meals went on for three days. Our boys bordered on hostility and aggression after being denied their normal caloric intake for that long. Cereal with warm milk, peanut butter and jelly, apples, gorp, tuna fish, and crackers pretty well lost all appeal early on the second day.

The night before our departure, I stopped to check our bill with the front desk clerk. As I turned to leave, she said pleasantly, "May I make your breakfast reservation in the hotel dining room tomorrow morning before you leave for the airport?" Not understanding, I asked her to explain. "Of course, *all of your meals were included in your room fee.*" In a millisecond, it all became clear. The reason the hotel was so expensive was that our meals were included in the price of the room. We had just spent three days eating the most awful food I could remember, when we could have been eating in the beautiful hotel dining room with all the other happy guests. The bitter irony was that we had to leave for the airport the next morning before the restaurant opened, so we even missed the one meal that we still had coming.

It would be great if I could say that I made up this story to make a point, but I didn't. Everyone does stupid things, but the Portugal trip is on my top ten list.

We all know people who are skilled at the art of living. They figure out in advance when the meals are included in the hotel stay. They always seem to know what to say, what to do, and what to wear. They're good at relating to other people and get themselves out of bad moods quickly. These individuals are also usually *wise at work*. They seem to get good jobs and get promoted more often. People like working for them; they work well on teams and always seem to know the best way to get something through the system. They have great self-management, good judgment, interpersonal effectiveness, and emotional stamina. They are perceptive about people and therefore make better hiring decisions. They tend to be more skilled in teamwork, collaboration, and conflict management. When they make a mistake, they bounce back with good humor and learn from the experience. When these individuals get promoted, there is a widespread emotional endorsement within the organization.

Undoubtedly, we know others who constantly stumble. They have a knack for saying the wrong thing. We all have clumsy moments, but these individuals are perpetually awkward. A cloud of gloom follows them around. They can be arrogant and often don't get the results their organization needs. They don't seem to learn from their mistakes and tend to deflect the feedback that is so necessary to improve at work. They lack good practical judgment or "horse sense." For example, I am amazed by how many people in customer service jobs lack basic judgment in handling customers. Many times big problems evaporate when a customer service agent makes a small, conciliatory gesture toward the customer. The person who exhibits good judgment is refreshing, and employers long for associates who manage themselves well and are good at dealing with others. In rare circumstances, organizations tolerate "interpersonal train wrecks," who are brilliant technically such as the "personality challenged" character, Chloe O'Brian, on the legendary TV series, 24. But more often, the price for keeping these types of individuals in the organization is too costly.

Competence—our ability to perform effectively in the work setting—is in large measure a product of skills and seven Critical Success Factors (CSFs). Both skills *and* CSFs are essential for those who aspire to achieve exceptional performance in their work. Skills make us competent for specific jobs such as selling, managing, accounting, analyzing, teaching, repairing an engine, building, flying a plane, restoring the ligaments in an injured knee, or making a presentation. Skills enable us to be hired for a specific job, and they are necessary for success; however, skills alone are insufficient.

We have all seen people who are exceptionally skilled and yet fail to achieve larger success in the work setting. Most of those individuals who fail at their jobs are deficient in one or more of the seven Critical Success Factors (CSFs).

Universal in nature, CSFs undergird the use of our skills and are essential for excellent performance in all jobs. Skills get us into the race, CSFs help us win it. My experience with thousands of individuals in the workplace convinced me that mastering seven CSFs is nonnegotiable for success.

Most universities or job training programs teach us skills instead of CSFs. Fortunately, these seven CSFs—self-management, relationship management, forethought, dependability, resourcefulness, ability to learn, ability to change—can be developed. Detailed discussion on each follows in the remaining chapters. Self-assessment exercises and developmental applications for the seven CSFs are found online at **runwiththebulls.net**.

CRITICAL SUCCESS FACTOR 1: SELF-MANAGEMENT

Individuals who are smart in a textbook sense have a high intelligence quotient or IQ. They can solve complex problems and are often quite logical.

Much of what we might recognize as effectiveness at living, scholars now call emotional intelligence or EQ, which includes the ability to manage one's self and effectively relate to others. People with a high EQ are also effective at controlling their impulses and managing the stress that can compromise moods and diminish empathy for others.

In a cover story on emotional intelligence, *Time* magazine looked at the IQ and EQ of different US presidents.[1] President Jimmy Carter, a Naval Academy graduate and submarine officer, is high on the IQ scale while President Ronald Reagan's IQ is thought to be above average but not at the top.

Although Carter's IQ is higher, he had trouble relating to his constituents—an EQ problem. Carter had a dour personality and often frowned. He told the citizens of the United States that they were in a slump, and he couldn't get the American economic engine to perform.

By contrast, many people of different political ideologies admired Reagan. He communicated in soaring themes that inspired Americans to believe in themselves, and his vision for American productivity fostered one of the greatest economic expansions in history. Reagan had a cheerful, upbeat personality, and his photos almost always showed him smiling. Even after John Hinckley tried to assassinate him, he joked with his surgeons about their political affiliations on the way to the operating room to have the bullet removed. Clearly, Reagan's EQ made him an endearing leader to millions worldwide.

Having recognized that IQ is not the sole determining factor in effectiveness, researchers have focused more in recent years on the emotional intelligence of high-achieving workers. An important adage has emerged in the workplace: "IQ gets you hired . . . EQ gets you promoted." That makes a lot of sense. To get in the door of most companies, we have to demonstrate some level of mental capacity (IQ), but once hired, the ability to manage our own behavior and our relationships with others (EQ) will likely have a greater impact on our success.

EQ deficits routinely undermine worker's effectiveness. A friend on the west coast recently experienced checking account fraud but didn't catch the irregularities for six weeks because he was traveling internationally. The amount of money involved was relatively small, particularly in light of how much money he kept in multiple business and personal accounts. My friend missed the bank's deadline for reporting the problem by a few days and then called his private banking representative in Los Angeles to enlist his help. Even though my friend was a very good customer, the bank's representative put on a formal "this is our policy" voice and politely told him that he'd missed the deadline and must forfeit the loss normally covered by the bank. Wrong answer. What he didn't know was that his client knew a senior officer four levels above him, who, upon hearing about the fraud, quickly restored my friend's stolen money to his account. Surprisingly, the rep became very stiff and formal in subsequent conversations. My friend said it would have taken only the slightest overture of warmth and goodwill to have him back in his corner. Yet the banker apparently was unable to mask his anger about a customer going over his head, and it further diminished their relationship. His poor reading of his customer and lack of judgment in handling the situation jeopardized a highly valued client's relationship with the bank.

IQ gets you hired . . .
EQ gets you promoted.

It is fascinating how self-management and good judgment show up very early in life. Daniel Goleman reported a study in his groundbreaking book, *Emotional Intelligence*, which illustrates the battle we all feel between impulse and restraint. A number of four-year-olds were placed in a room with an experimenter, who left for a few minutes. Before leaving the room, the experimenter explained to each child that he or she could eat one marshmallow left on a plate while he was gone. However, if the child waited until the experimenter returned, he or she could have a second marshmallow. We can probably picture ourselves in that situation. Some ate the marshmallow within seconds of the experimenter leaving the room. Others waited and waited and . . . the children who waited hid their eyes or distracted themselves in other ways, but they managed to wait. Twelve and fifteen years later, the same children were tested on a number of different measures, and the results were dramatic. The children who waited for the second marshmallow scored higher than their peers in the following areas when they were tested as high school seniors:

- Social competence
- Assertiveness
- Ability to cope with the frustrations of life

- Resilience under stress
- Self-reliance
- Confidence
- Dependability
- Initiative
- Ability to delay gratification
- Success in school
- SATs (210-point average difference)

Of particular interest to scientists was that the marshmallow test was twice as good a predictor of these children's eventual SAT scores as IQ.[2] However, even if we were in the immediate gratification group, there is substantial research supporting the conclusion that self-control and interpersonal skills can be acquired as adults. We can actually learn to wait on the second marshmallow. How we change and grow is the main subject of a later chapter, so the following are some of the practical actions these effective people take.

IS HE TALKING TO HIMSELF?

Learning to be wise at work requires a tremendous range of self-management, which begins with self-awareness. Being emotionally self-aware is essential for the control and healthy directing of emotions, especially negative or disruptive emotions such as anger. Accurate self-awareness is essential to change and dealing with weaknesses.

A prerequisite for doing something about how we feel is to know what we feel and why we feel that way. It's those undefined "bad" feelings that get us in trouble.

Self-awareness is a hallmark of emotionally intelligent individuals. Do you ever wake up grumpy and aren't sure why? It may be that you were worried about a presentation at work and didn't sleep well. It could be the rumors about layoffs or a host of other things. A prerequisite for doing something about how we feel is to know *what we feel and why we feel that way*. It's those undefined "bad" feelings that get us in trouble. We carry them with us, and they spill over into our interactions with others. Our coworkers see us frowning or sending off negative vibes, so they try to steer clear and avoid being pulled down into our negative state.

Many of the people we most admire have regular private conversations with themselves that go something like this:

OK, so I don't feel so hot. I should have gone to bed earlier last night instead of watching *Star Wars* for the fifth time. I'm not quite ready for the weekend to be over, and I think I have a case of "Monday morning flu." OK. I need to go for a run, eat some protein, and remember that it really was a great weekend. There's a lot of important stuff happening today, most of which I need to be "up" for. The presentation for the new order fulfillment system is huge, and my boss's boss will be there. My goal is to make this the best presentation I've ever made. I'm just going to have to grab myself by the nape of the neck and pull myself out of this funk. I'm going to think positively and remember that unbelievable sunset we saw at the lake on Saturday night. The first thing I'm going to do at work is check on my team, greet them warmly, and thank them for their hard work last week in getting the presentation finalized. Although John is dragging us down—nope, I'm not going there this morning—it can wait. Julie deserves a medal of honor for working over the weekend to get the presentation ready. The team's work is stellar, and I think it's going to be obvious why we need to change the system. I am going to smile and say, "Good morning," to everyone I see, especially the grouch at the reception desk. I'm also going to do one more dry run on the presentation, make sure the visuals are working, and get the timing down better on the final two slides . . .

You might be saying, "Nobody talks to themselves like this." Well, actually they do—especially the successful ones. They tone down negative emotions and take steps to get physically in tune. They plan actions that will generate positive feelings. They give away what they need themselves such as affirmation. They rehearse actions that are important to increase their confidence. They smile even when they don't exactly feel like smiling. By the way, poor performers also have self-talk—it's just negative or even catastrophic in nature. Their self-talk expects the worst, and they typically get it.

High performers remain self-aware and then connect feelings, especially bad ones, to a rational cause. The emotionally intelligent person then takes steps to move past negative emotions and rehearse the big events of the day. Sometimes the rehearsal is real time, and sometimes it's just mental. Performance psychologists view rehearsal as a critical step in high achievement.

EMOTIONAL SELF-MANAGEMENT

Managing ourselves is probably life's greatest challenge. It includes everything from simply getting to work on time to the complexity of controlling what we say. We all have bad days. Successful people grab hold of themselves emotionally and manage their way out. They conquer negative impulses and resist overreacting. What aspects of emotional self-management are most important in the workplace?

> *Emotionally intelligent people do not suppress the awareness of negative emotions, but they do moderate the expression of feelings to the right level of intensity or the right time.*

Optimism. Martin Seligman, a professor at the University of Pennsylvania, identified optimism as the number one contributor to success in many areas.[3] We typically don't like to be around people who are naïvely optimistic, but we do like to work with people who focus on the upside. Successful people find reasons for optimism. They expect the best out of others. You may have heard a joke President Reagan was fond of telling. When he saw a big pile of horse manure, he quipped, "There has to be a pony in there somewhere."

Control of Negative Emotions. Aristotle said, "Anyone can become angry—that is easy. But to be angry with the right person, to the right degree, at the right time, for the right purpose, and in the right way—that is not easy."[4] Emotionally intelligent people do not suppress the *awareness* of negative emotions, but they do moderate the *expression* of feelings to the right level of intensity or the right time. This is especially critical in the workplace. A New Testament writer tells us, "Everyone should be quick to listen, slow to speak and slow to become angry."[5] This is very practical advice for us in dealing with our colleagues—make sure you understand the full scope of the problem before you respond.

Assertiveness. Assertiveness is probably best understood in contrast with aggressiveness. Assertiveness is firmly taking a stand on an issue without demeaning the other person, while aggressiveness tries to take down the other person's argument and the other person at the same time. Successful individuals take purposeful steps to advance their agenda, and if in a leadership role, they work with their teams to organize solutions to difficult problems. They are intentional and take the initiative instead of waiting passively for solutions. They also speak candidly about their opinions and feelings. Assertive individuals more often use the word *I,* in order to establish their own position. Aggressive individuals tend to use the word *you* in a way that attempts to diminish the position of others.

Stress Tolerance. Stress is normal and certain to be present in the workplace. Moderate stress actually boosts our performance, but there is a precipitous drop in our performance when stress gets too high. Stress-tolerant individuals monitor their stress levels and find ways to diminish their stress before it impacts their effectiveness. When stress causes negative emotions, they find ways to reduce the stress to a more reasonable level. High achievers remain calmer under stress; they're less impulsive and have a greater ability to tolerate pressure. Their higher adaptability in stressful situations provides them with solutions unavailable to individuals preoccupied with fear and anxiety.

High Expectations. High achievers expect a lot from themselves and others. They set the bar high and allay any negativity that interferes with the goal. They push their teams to higher standards and tough but realistic, achievable goals. Fifty percent of workers say they do not put effort into their jobs over and above what is required to hold it.[6] A man once mentioned to me that his father told him while he was growing up that he should never do more work than he had to. This young man's quality bar was set so low that it was obvious why his new business was having trouble. We should always be pushing ourselves toward excellence.

Verbal Self-Management

An additional aspect of self-management involves what we say and don't say. Although it's normal on occasion to blurt out things that we later wish we hadn't said, we often feel the pain and remorse when we've said something we can't take back. Some of our coworkers have chronic "foot-in-mouth" disease, but once a verbal misstep is out there, the damage is done.

It's important to remember how powerful our words can be. One sage observer compares our tongues to a match that can set fire to a whole forest. A similar analogy compares the tongue to the rudder of a ship—a small object can steer a very large one.[7] What we say has great power for good or bad.

If you're new to a job, be careful of what you say, particularly in the early months. It's important to learn the organization's mores: the traditions, the taboos, and the unwritten rules. Organizational politics impacts our successes in most organizations, and it's far too easy to unintentionally make a critical comment about someone's pet project. It's like telling someone, "Your baby is ugly." Not a career-advancing move.

Sometimes the things we blurt out just can't be contained. In the comedy *Liar, Liar,* Jim Carrey plays attorney Fletcher Reede, who frequently lies to get out of his commitments. His son makes a birthday wish that his father will tell the truth for the next twenty-four hours, and Reede's attempts to stifle his comments create some major contortions. We all struggle with those impulses, but high achievers typically rein them in and censor what shouldn't be spoken.

It's always fascinating to study the participants in a meeting. A few state the obvious. Some meander through tangled, meaningless garble, while others in the meeting look dazed, bored, or confused. Then there's the speaker who adds clarity to the matter at hand. The group's energy goes up, the conversation is revitalized, and often the understanding of the problem advances dramatically. There is almost nothing better than words wisely spoken.

Being wise at work involves being open and candid. Sometimes direct, honest communication is exactly what's called for, while in some situations discretion is needed. Wisdom recognizes the difference. Before speaking, ask yourself: "Does this comment add value? Is it going to help us understand a problem or create a better solution?" If the answer is not a clear yes, then sit on your statement for a while.

Do you work with someone who talks too much? One person I've observed talks so much and so often that others on his team mentally shut down whenever he says anything. This guy's long-windedness defeats any hope he has of being effective. Any valuable points he may make are lost in the verbiage.

A wise person makes his words count. His speech is concise and focuses on creating clear understanding for the listener. Those who speak in a meeting with the greatest impact usually speak a few apt words in a calm manner. I consistently observe these effective contributors sit back and listen to a discussion for a few minutes. They take a few notes on what's being said. They organize their thoughts, and when they eventually speak, their words cut through the haze like fog lights.

> *A wise person makes his words count. His speech is concise and focuses on creating clear understanding for the listener.*

THE BLUE SUITCASE REVISITED

Our problem on the trip to Portugal was rooted in a lack of awareness. Eating in the beautiful dining room was our privilege—it came with the room. We simply didn't know what we had, so we didn't take advantage of it.

Many people are eating out of a blue suitcase at work with no awareness they could be eating in the dining room, so each day is a poor substitute for what could have been. Work is a painful place in which success and significance are illusory. These individuals maintain low expectations of themselves and usually meet them. They're constantly stressed out and never seem to have effective relationships at work.

Instead, we can eat in the dining room. Work should help us find meaning and significance. Of course, we make money, which provides for ourselves and others, but it should also be a place in which the best in us comes out. Self-management means using our unique skills to serve our customers and coworkers and reach important goals.

Self-management is Critical Success Factor 1, and everything else rests on top of this fundamental building block. Achievement is rooted in self-awareness, which supports the choices we must make every day to be optimistic, control our negative emotions, be assertive, manage stress, maintain high expectations, and regulate our speech. Not that simple, and definitely not easy.

9

Run Well with Others

*I have come to the frightening conclusion
that I am the decisive element.*
—Johann Wolfgang von Goethe, 1749–1832

My father passed on to me his love of the western United States. Many of my best memories are from our vacations driving around Colorado, Montana, Wyoming, Utah, California, and Oregon. The scale of the geologic features and vistas out West still awes me.

When a friend invited me to bring my sons on a one-week backpacking trip in the wilderness near Yosemite National Park, I jumped at the chance. All the dads and their kids hiked to a base camp at about 8,000 feet with extraordinary views of the surrounding mountains. Our guides were seasoned outdoor leaders and hard-core environmentalists committed to no-impact incursions to the back country. We left nothing behind— literally everything we brought in came out with us at the end of the week. One young camper dropped a flake from a granola bar and planned to leave it on the ground. Not only did the kid have to eat the flake, but the event became a "learning module" on why chipmunks should never, ever taste sugar.

The days were filled with training in rock climbing and rappelling mixed with dad/kid bonding time. We faced numerous challenges during the week, such as climbing sheer rock walls and cleaning our cooking utensils with sand and gravel—no detergents permitted in the wilderness. The graduation exercise was to rappel off "the Prow," so named because the silhouette of the huge rock formation looked like the prow of an old sailing ship.

The face of the Prow jutted out into an expanse so vast you could see for hundreds of miles in every direction. Our task was to rappel down to a narrow path 160 feet below the top of the rock. After the first fifty feet, it became a "free rappel" when the rock's surface cut back away from the vertical line, leaving the rappeller dangling in midair.

Because the narrow path lay tucked underneath the enormous rock, all we could see from the top of the Prow was the canyon floor a thousand feet below. The anticipation of hanging that far above the ground on a small rope almost made me hyperventilate. The guides checked and rechecked my rigging and made sure my "eight ring," the metal device for controlling the speed of decent, worked smoothly. As an additional safety precaution, one of the guides tied a second rope around my waist to "belay" me, should the main rope fail.

As I backed down the face of the rock, more and more of my weight rested on the rope. The guides warned me that I would see a line scratched into the face of the rock, called the "point of no return." This mark indicated the point at which I could not back out. It would be impossible for me to get back up the face of the rock from below that threshold.

Upon reaching the point of no return, I looked over my shoulder at the canyon floor. My surging adrenaline made me almost hallucinogenic with anxiety. From our training earlier in the week, I understood the mechanics of rappelling. My rational understanding of the friction created by the eight ring to slow my speed became instantly superfluous. Raw, naked fear now overwhelmed any attempt at reason.

My foot not making contact with rock told me I was now going into the free rappel, and as I took that final step into space, my mind flashed to a horrifying thought: the guy holding the rope, to whom I had entrusted my life should something go wrong, had no hands! A congenital birth defect had left Mark with nothing but partial forearms.

Mark was an extraordinary person in many respects. He had overcome his disability so spectacularly that his absence of hands had minimal impact. He was an academic All-American, and his record for number of tackles in a season still stands on the college football team for whom he started as a linebacker during his junior and senior years. Despite his obvious expertise, my confidence still wavered.

The wind began to blow me from side to side, making me almost nauseated with vertigo. In a foolish move, I looked over my shoulder and then froze. The height made me so dizzy, my brain shut down. Suddenly Mark sang out, "Tim, you're looking good. Don't worry, I've got you. Just let out some more rope. Don't make me come get you!"

His laughter did the trick. My brain rebooted. Another twenty or thirty feet, and I actually began to enjoy the rappel. I saw the canyon below and the river in the distance from that incredible perspective, and a few minutes later the path felt unbelievably good under my feet.

I later climbed back to the top of the Prow to watch Mark belay other rappellers. He had created an amazing system by wrapping the rope around his waist and using his arms as brakes. His adaptation worked flawlessly.

WHY DO PEOPLE GET FIRED?

Despite technology, virtual offices, and new ways of getting work done, the workplace is more interdependent than ever. No matter what size organization we work for, we must work with others, and our ability to work well with others has a gigantic impact on how well we do our jobs. Critical Success Factor 2, Relationship Management, is a major key to effectiveness in the workplace. Being wise at work requires that we learn to work effectively with others. More often than not, we need help from others in the workplace over whom we have no authority. Skillful relationship management relies on the influence gained from knowing people, understanding differences, and recognizing conflicting agendas. Skillfully managing relationships with our boss, our peers, our direct reports, or our customers can make or break a career.

How well you work with others determines how effectively you perform in the workplace. Competence spans not only the accomplishment of the task but also how you collaborate with others in the accomplishment of that task. Working on a team, managing conflict effectively, and influencing others can spell the difference between success and failure in today's workplace.

> *How well you work with others determines how effectively you perform in the workplace. Competence spans not only the accomplishment of the task but also how you collaborate with others in the accomplishment of that task.*

We are all working around our own imperfections and dealing with the imperfections of others. While they may not be as physically obvious as Mark's, they're just as profound—if not more so—in their impact on our behavior. Fundamentally, working with others is rooted in the trust of imperfect people.

Among the many people I have worked with, very few have been fired for lack of technical skills. Certainly, some people I have interviewed are not hired because they lack the right technical skills for a given job, and being fired for this reason is rare because technical qualifications are relatively easy to verify. It's more often poor relationship skills that get people fired.

The Apprentice provides rich examples of this reality. One 2005 episode showed two teams creating an action figure to help brand a well-known fast-food restaurant. Neither of the teams produced a world-class figure, but the team that won worked together much more effectively. Their figure included more of the critical elements that a marketing buyer looks for, such as easy brand identification; however, that was not what won the competition. The team that won had fun, they collaborated well, and their energy in the presentation was infectious. The two buyers from the restaurant chain looked up, smiled, and joined in their laughter.

> *We are all working around our own imperfections . . . fundamentally, working with others is rooted in the trust of imperfect people.*

The team that lost actually had more technical ability among the team members than the team that won. The losing team fell apart in the preparation. If I had been Donald Trump, it would have been hard to decide who to fire, because the whole team was dysfunctional. The woman Trump chose to let go destroyed the team's unity. She was arrogant. (On the post-firing taxi ride she said, "I wouldn't hire any of those other women to be my executive assistant.") She lied to the team about why she didn't do what the team requested of her. Her failure to work with the team diminished their creativity, and her toxic manner prevented others from being honest about the flaws in their product. During the presentation, the losing team lacked confidence, and it became apparent that their design failed to address several critical market needs that they hadn't even thought about in their preparation. Although quite polite, the buyers looked down and frowned. The team stumbled while answering questions. Afterwards, Trump told his two associates that he hated to fire the woman, because she was the smartest in the group. She just couldn't get along with her teammates.

CRITICAL SUCCESS FACTOR 2: RELATIONSHIP MANAGEMENT

Successful individuals focus on having good *relationships* with others rather than good *friendships*. Good relationships at work occur because of how we manage those relationships, while friendships tend to be a matter of chemistry. If you end up being friends with someone at work, fine, but some of the best relationships on the job can actually be with people we don't especially like. People who are highly skilled at relationship management often manifest several common attributes when relating to others.

> *In our work relationships, it helps to assume that others have positive motives.*

ASSUME POSITIVE MOTIVES

Most people operate out of self-interest, but they also want their organization to reach its goals and to do well; they want to work for an organization they're proud of. They want to get along with others. Most want to do a good job.

Therefore, in our work relationships, it helps to assume that others have positive motives. Assumptions act like filters that influence how we hear and, in turn, react to the words and actions of others. When we assume the best, we are more trusting, more generous, and more likely to help others succeed. The recipients of these actions often reciprocate and put their trust in us.

While it's potentially naïve to assume that all of our colleagues have positive motives, especially toward us, it still helps the relationship to treat the other individual as if he or she means well. One savvy executive told me that, "I treat others as if they had positive motives even when I know they do not, because it often helps the relationship." Treating others as if they had positive motives becomes an action of strength. Even our enemies sometimes act with more integrity.

EMPATHIZE

The wise person understands that everyone has a valuable story to be told—and is, therefore, a patient, empathetic listener. The most effective executives with whom I've worked ask great questions and listen carefully to the people who work with them. They take notes, they make eye contact, and they show interest in what the speaker is saying. They ask questions and listen for understanding, often summarizing what others have said. At first they listen uncritically but then ask perceptive questions that help everyone better grasp the issues. Most importantly, these skilled relaters *listen for understanding while not necessarily agreeing with what the other person said.* They show thoughtful consideration for the opinions of others without affirming their correctness. They are discerning. Empathy conveys an interest in the other person's problem, not an automatic seconding of their solution.

In the workplace we sometimes see the most effective displays of empathy among excellent salespeople. They put themselves inside a customer's world to understand how that customer experiences an opportunity or challenge. They listen to their customers, ask questions about their needs, and empathize with their problems long before they start pitching their product or service. There is a very powerful disarming effect to empathy: it allows the other person to feel understood and to relax.

I frequently hear managers label salespeople as "product pushers." This is not a flattering reference. A product pusher is a salesperson who goes to his customer with an agenda: not to hear his customer but to be heard by the customer. We also see agenda pushers inside our organizations. They don't listen to us or anyone else, and we always have the sense that they are focused only on their own agenda. Getting clear about the other person's needs before we launch into what we want is a great tactic for sales. Empathy works the same way inside organizations, because it's a great tool for building trust and collaboration with our colleagues at work.

> *Answering before listening*
> *is both stupid and rude.*
> —KING SOLOMON[1]

If you want to get along well with your boss, try to put yourself in his or her shoes—show empathy for the person to whom you report. If you look at the world through your boss's eyes, what are the biggest concerns he or she might have? An executive client often told his management team, "Give me my bad news early." What did he mean by that? He was telling his team about his biggest concern. Essentially, he was asking his colleagues to alert him to major problems early enough so that he could help solve the problem. By getting involved early, he could use his unique capabilities or the power of his senior position to help resolve the problem. He found it intensely frustrating not to know about a crucial problem when he could have made a difference had he been alerted earlier.

Another aspect of empathy is being sure you communicate early and often if your actions impact others. Your colleagues may like to be surprised on their birthdays, but they don't like being surprised about work —make sure you communicate extensively when your actions or decisions affect what others may be doing in your organization. Think about the times you were disadvantaged or unprepared when someone didn't tell you about a change that impacted you and your colleagues. How did you feel? Remember those occurrences and your empathy level will rise.

HANDLE CONFLICT SKILLFULLY

Conflict permeates most workplaces, so if you want to be effective, learn to handle conflict well. Dealing with conflict promptly is foundational. Much of the ill will in organizations stems from the "elephantlike" memories of coworkers who are still resentful about past slights. When leaders from different departments are at odds, it is easy to let bitterness take hold, and then everyone takes sides. Two warring departments can be particularly ugly, dragging everyone involved into a toxic waste dump.

Conflict becomes more manageable when we own our own stuff. Any time we automatically assume that it's completely the other person's fault, we probably need to do a gut check on how we may be contributing to the impasse. Be open to criticism from others. Acknowledging our contribution to a conflict or problem can be very effective in unfreezing communication with a colleague at work. We are powerless to control a coworker's response, but we can at least demonstrate integrity in our own actions, such as apologizing for our part in a problem.

In a conflict, it is very normal for one entity's interests to be pitted against another's. Some of my staff were at loggerheads with a client over a major project. The client wanted a lower price for the work, and my staff said that what we were being asked to do far exceeded the existing price. This very important project was close to blowing up, embarrassing the client with her internal sponsors and hurting my team's reputation and revenue.

The project leader very wisely talked to the client and refocused the discussion on shared problems. The scope of work and everyone's roles needed to be clearer. The project leader and the lead representative for the client agreed to a summit during which they could team up against the problem. The effort was effective because the client became aware of how much the consultants were actually doing for her and realized that much of it should be done internally by members of her team.

The key to the success of the summit was that they de-escalated the tension by shifting the focus away from one entity's interests being opposed to the other's. By joining forces against the problem, they deflated the natural tendency to point fingers and say, "What are you going to do to fix this?" Vendor and consultant each accepted responsibility for 100 percent of the problem, and had the courage to say so. Each took on the responsibility to find a solution, and this joining together of resources generated answers that could not have been reached in a finger-pointing environment. The quote by Goethe at the beginning of the chapter acknowledges the risk we take when we view ourselves as responsible. Many problems in the workplace would go away if more people stepped up and said, "I am going to be a decisive element in making this organization work."

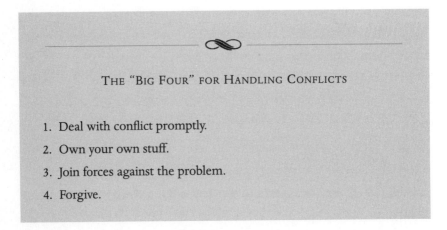

THE "BIG FOUR" FOR HANDLING CONFLICTS

1. Deal with conflict promptly.
2. Own your own stuff.
3. Join forces against the problem.
4. Forgive.

FORGIVE

Although I have had the privilege of observing many great companies, I have also seen some that were absolutely toxic, rooted in a culture of personal injury. The backstabbings, the slights, and the decisions made for any number of ridiculous reasons other than merit all contribute to workplace toxicity. Just as we can see on *The Apprentice* (and other reality shows), people sometimes viciously turn on each other.

Forgiveness seems like an odd subject to apply to the workplace. Many think that only wimps apologize or forgive; showing weaknesses to workplace adversaries invites other attacks. Actually, forgiveness in the workplace has become the subject of serious scientific research. Psychologists such as Dr. Everett Worthington, a psychology professor at Virginia Commonwealth University, are actively researching the benefits of forgiveness. When woven into the fabric of corporate culture, the benefits are substantial. Dr. Worthington mentions better relationships and better health, to name a few.[2]

One senior executive of a well-known Fortune 100 company went against the counsel of the company's CEO and invested $10 million in an ill-fated marketing campaign for a new consumer product venture. As the CEO predicted, the campaign bombed. The senior executive went to see his boss, fully expecting to be fired. Instead, the CEO shot back, "Fire you? What do you mean fire you? We just invested $10 million in your training program." This humbled senior executive learned from his mistake and actually went on to be CEO some years later.

Forgiveness is a powerful experience in the workplace and in life. It's healing; it restores trust and brings health to our relationships at work. When leaders admit their mistakes and humbly request forgiveness, the team increases its respect and commitment.

Sadly, when two members of a team allow a root of bitterness to grow up in their relationship, it affects the whole team. We're all aware of when there is hostility between people. In meetings, it's like the "dead cat under the table." Everyone knows it's there, but no one will acknowledge it. The bitterness saps energy from the team and its work.

Just as an organization can be toxic in its management practices or culture, individuals sometimes exhibit toxic behavior. They seem to get satisfaction out of nursing a grudge. They feel righteous from being wronged, and their inevitable victim status makes these types of people feel magnanimous. Hanging on to their slight is safer than forgiving their perceived enemy and having to reengage with him. It's hard to know exactly what to do in that situation. It may be best to simply forgive the person, treat them respectfully, but also maintain the distance that the other person seems to want. Ultimately, we have no control over how someone else responds. No relationship is perfect, but we should always seek to act with integrity and good will.

Integrity, competence, and effective relationships are the ingredients that form the trust on which all work is effectively conducted.

GOOD RELATIONSHIPS ARE NEITHER SIMPLE NOR EASY

Relationships are our work life's most complex dimension, but they are one of the Critical Success Factors. When we think about work—our accomplishments, our challenges, our hopes, and our concerns—most of the time it involves other people. Integrity, competence, and effective relationships are the ingredients that form the trust on which all work is effectively conducted.

Having solid relationships requires effort and focus. The good ones truly have to be built over time. The most important building blocks are assuming positive motives, showing empathy, handling conflict skillfully, and forgiving. These actions are complex and difficult but essential for success at work.

10

Run with Skill

Bob: *If you would, would you walk us through a typical day for you?*

Peter: *Yeah.*

Bob: *Great.*

Peter: *Well, I generally come in at least fifteen minutes late, ah, I use the side door—that way Lumberg can't see, heh—after that I sorta space out for an hour.*

Consultant: *Da-uh? Space out?*

Peter: *Yeah, I just stare at my desk, but it looks like I'm working. I do that for probably another hour after lunch too. I'd say in a given week I probably only do about fifteen minutes of real, actual work.*

—Scene from *Office Space* (20th Century Fox), 1999

We traversed the Amazon rainforest in a small boat, as rain-swollen streams had transformed the area into a vast waterway. Wild tropical orchids covered everything in sight, their spectacular purple blossoms like ubiquitous kudzu vines on an abandoned south Georgia farm. Indigenous people in dugout canoes hunting fish with spears peered at us silently in the shadows of vines and ancient, towering trees. Screeching monkeys protested our trespass, and the dense canopy overhead blocked most of the sun, trapping what must be the most extreme humidity on the planet.

A few years ago, a client organization asked me to facilitate their leadership meeting in Pucallpa, Peru, a sparse frontier town near the headwaters of the Amazon River, which Anne, the boys, and I navigated during our afternoon free time. The organization owned several corporate aircraft and agreed to fly us to Cusco, Peru, to tour Machu Picchu, the famous Inca ruins. What I didn't know was that to fly over the Peruvian Andes, we would travel in a small single-engine plane in which each passenger donned an oxygen mask at 14,000 feet to prevent hypoxia in the nonpressurized cabin (our pilot put on his mask at 11,000 feet as an added safety measure). When we arrived at the grass landing strip, Anne gave me a number of those unhappy sideways looks that said, "What have you gotten us into this time?"

When we arrived at the grass landing strip, Anne gave me a number of those unhappy sideways looks that said, "What have you gotten us into this time?"

Actually, I felt surprisingly safe under the circumstances. Dave, our somewhat laconic pilot, had logged thousands of hours of flight time in demanding conditions, flying government officials, medical personnel, linguists, and other officially approved passengers deep into the jungle. His grilling of the mechanics about that morning's routine maintenance and careful review of the critical preflight checklists let us know he was highly competent and clearly in charge of this flight.

The sunny ascent over the vast green expanse of jungle was magnificent. We followed one of the huge tributaries of the Amazon southwest toward the Andes, but not long into the flight, conditions changed dramatically when we entered a thick cloud bank. After an hour of flying on instruments in zero visibility, Dave looked pensive and observed,

"I think the engine is not getting enough air because of an ice buildup on the manifold intake. This prevents the engine from generating adequate power to reach the necessary altitude." Ironically, at the same moment, he adjusted a valve on the bulkhead and a handful of ice dropped into the cabin. He responded, "I'm not sure why we have ice in that vent." Behind her clear plastic oxygen mask, Anne looked like she was going to faint, and I read her thoughts—"The engine is dying, and the wings are iced over. The plane will soon crash in a jungle so vast and dense that a search crew will not even bother looking for us." She explained later that our family being together was her only comfort: no one would be orphaned.

Dave calmly turned and commented, "Hey, everything's fine. The engine's not getting enough air, but all we need to do is get to a lower elevation and melt the ice. This requires that we land on an alternate airstrip to get more fuel before continuing our trip." He further explained that the landing would be a bit unusual because the grass runway was uphill!

A few minutes later we landed on an uphill strip literally carved out of the side of a mountainous jungle. As we taxied over to a clearing, Dave commented, "There has been some activity in the southern region of Peru by a terrorist group called *Sendero Luminoso* (The Shining Path), but, rest assured, we would never fly you into an area that is considered unsafe. The only other concern is that if anyone has taken our fuel, we'll be going back to Pucallpa on a river barge, which takes about a week." Just as Dave killed the engine, about thirty people appeared from nowhere, certain to be the very terrorists Dave had just warned us about. Anne prayed what she knew were her final prayers before our family was taken captive or killed by terrorists.

Dave greeted and hugged a few of the local villagers who stored and watched over his gas. They helped him roll a fifty-five-gallon barrel of fuel from a nearby hut to the plane and watched him refuel the plane's gas tanks one bucketful at a time while standing on a shaky stepladder.

This time the plane reached the required altitude, and we crossed the Andes just a thousand feet above the spectacularly jagged peaks. Unfortunately, on the other side of the Andes, the weather continued to deteriorate, and Dave's face showed the strain of the long flight. Everyone on board desperately prayed for an opening in the cloud cover. We flew on in silence until Dave commented, "I have sometimes found a break in the clouds over one section of Cusco." A few minutes later, we looked into the distance, and an oval-shaped hole about a half-mile wide loomed almost directly over Cusco's airport. As we dipped through the clouds, locals in their colorful wool clothing hurried off the runway, leading their pack animals.

This flight was harrowing. Although there are always risks in flying, they were much more evident in a small, single-engine plane than on a 767. The success of our cross-jungle flight rested in the hands of a highly competent pilot. Some of the best bush pilots in the world trained him for jungle flying; he practiced landings under the worst possible conditions and had two options for every scenario they threw at him.

Certain unique, specialized skills undergirded Dave's effectiveness. He clearly had mastered the necessary skills of flying the airplane, including the mechanics, the navigational systems, and the other complex avionics. While these skills were essential for flying safely, there were other competencies that made Dave truly effective at his job.

AIRDAVE

Although Dave was one of a number of the organization's pilots who routinely flew this particular airplane, he treated it like it was his own—

we could have been flying "AirDave." That morning our pilot was the president of AirDave, and he was in charge of getting us to Cusco safely. He accepted responsibility for getting us to our destination not only physically intact, but also emotionally in one piece—it was his job to reassure his nervous passengers.

Our pilot was also resourceful and prepared for the unexpected. He'd sent the fifty-five-gallon drum of fuel up the river on a barge two weeks prior to our flight just in case we needed it—he prepared for the contingency that eventually occurred. Dave quickly sized up the icing problem and took decisive action to remedy it. Though the conditions were stressful, he worked his backup plan to thaw the manifold intake and refuel. After hitting the cloud bank, it would have been easy for Dave to declare the conditions unfit for flying and return to base, but he used every resource available to get us to our destination: he had a "finish-line mentality." Within the bounds of safety, Dave intended to complete the task.

Dave excelled as a pilot because he never stopped learning about flying. He had just returned from the US, where he attended a flight school on advanced navigation. The bookshelves in his office bulged with flight books and technical magazines. He seemed to enjoy talking with his passengers about a wide range of subjects and asked me numerous thoughtful questions about my work. He had a captive audience, and his perceptive questions kept me talking about what he wanted to learn. Dave loved his work and excelled at it.

WE LOVE SEEING SOMEONE WHO'S GOOD

A house painter recently described to me in great detail how he was going to paint my front door in cooperation with how the wood had originally grown. Monet could not have held more reverence for a canvas than this painter had for that front door. It truly was a work of art when he finished. Watching a highly skilled person mesmerizes us: the flashing knives of a chef grilling at a table, the taxi driver who breezes through terrible traffic, the surgeon who makes a knee work like new, the IT person who fixes an ailing computer, the fishing guide whose picture-perfect casts make artistry out of a stretch of plastic line, the teacher who inspires us, or the designer who turns a room into a space so beautiful and serene, our heart slows its hectic pace.

Conversely, the truly incompetent, unskilled person brings us down to the depths of despair. Some of us feel like Edvard Munch's famous painting, *The Scream*, after being the recipient of incompetence. We dread that look in the repairperson's eyes that says, "Man, I really don't know what I'm doing."

It's particularly confusing when individuals who don't know what they're doing get promoted, especially when they are given a high-profile management job. As a manager, they're like Bill Lumbergh (played by Gary Cole) in *Office Space* in the quote at the beginning of this chapter. People hate working for them because everything these managers do and say is demotivating to their employees. Their promotion creates widespread incredulity. "Can you believe so-and-so got promoted? He's an absolute moron," is the comment heard in the break room.

> *Organizations value employees who are skilled because they provide the competitive edge in today's marketplace.*

Highly skilled, competent employees are rare and highly prized. Organizations value employees who are skilled because they provide *the* competitive edge in today's marketplace. Among the executives I've interviewed, many were smart and had great interpersonal skills, but ultimately the truly effective ones distinguished themselves by being good at what they did—they were competent. They achieved results in areas that mattered to the organizations they served.

MASTERY—THE SOURCE OF SELF-ESTEEM AT WORK

Our self-esteem is directly tied to our sense of mastery in our job. We want to be able to do the job we were hired to do—it's a great feeling when we do something well. By contrast, it's terrible when we feel like we're not doing a good job. It eats away at us night after night, and we wake up at 3:00 a.m. worrying about work. Our self-esteem takes a huge hit. We desperately want to hear that we're doing a good job but are full of angst that we're not.

Dr. Pauline Rose Clance's *The Imposter Syndrome* documents how even professionals with years of training and experience worry that they are frauds. We feel it is just a matter of time before we are discovered not to be the competent managers, teachers, or engineers that others believe us to be. It's like the old joke about a famous zoo that experienced budget cuts about the same time its star attraction—a gorilla—died. To save money, the zoo's superintendent persuaded an employee to wear a gorilla suit and sit in a cage; it fooled the public for a few weeks. One morning, the gorilla accidentally fell off a wall and into the lion's cage next door. Just as the man was about to scream for help, the lion leaned over and whispered, "Shut up, you fool, or we'll both be fired!" Most of us experience the imposter syndrome at one time or another and feel like a fake gorilla: we're just wearing the suit, waiting to be found out for who we really are—an imposter.

The last two chapters dealt with the first two Critical Success Factors (self-management and relationship management). This chapter will highlight four more CSFs that foster exceptional performance at work: forethought, dependability, resourcefulness, and ability to learn.

CRITICAL SUCCESS FACTOR 3: FORETHOUGHT

A recent *60 Minutes* interview featured Tom Brady, the sensational quarterback of the New England Patriots, who at age twenty-eight had already won three Super Bowls. Steve Kroft interviewed Brady and pointed out that he had none of the attributes associated with great quarterbacks. The NFL scouts viewed Brady as a mediocre talent in college and drafted him very late. What's the secret of his success? It's forethought. Brady spends a tremendous amount of time mentally preparing for the team's next game. He watches game films to visualize how his next game will unfold. The actual game is simply the execution of the plan already in his head. He told Kroft, "It's not like you just go out there and wing it . . . you try that, you're going to get hit and you're going to throw interceptions. And that's no way to play the game."[1]

Unfortunately, we sometimes do wing it, with predictable results—we get hit. Not long ago a staff member asked if I would meet with her and a potential client to discuss their need for some of our services. The date was four months out, so I agreed to the meeting and then forgot about it. The day of the meeting, I touched base with my staff member, and we walked through our strategy for the meeting. My staff member felt the meeting needed to be more social and less about presenting our services. After a great start, about halfway through the meeting the prospect began to ask questions that implied a certain level of forethought on our part. He asked if we had read the autobiography of the founder of his company, or if we had read recent analyst's reports evaluating their new strategy. We had not, and he nailed us. How could he take us seriously if we hadn't done our homework? He was right. Competence depends upon forethought—careful anticipation of what is needed to produce a good outcome. By the way, the next time we met with that potential client, I made sure I knew more about their company's founder than our prospect did.

Forethought is looking ahead. Dave possessed the unique skill of landing an airplane in difficult conditions, but it was his forethought (a skill that can be developed) that provided us with a supply of fuel to continue our trip. Wise workers are always looking ahead to identify possible problems or opportunities that can either hurt or help their efforts. The first step of any battle is to get the lay of the land—the scope and the challenges of the task. Sun Tzu also wrote, "We are not fit to lead an army on the march unless we are familiar with the face of the country—its mountains and forests, its pitfalls and precipices, its marshes and swamps.[2]

Few of us would ever just "wing it" on a road trip from Chicago to Philadelphia in January. However, most people jump into virtually every work task without considering what might be ahead. What preparation should you make for the following work assignments?

- You must make a presentation to a potential client on why the capabilities of your organization are well-suited to meet his needs.
- You must select a new curriculum for your class next year.
- You must recommend a new shipping company for your business.
- You are assigned to pick up a customer at the airport this afternoon.

The level of planning and preparation reflects the nature of the task, but even something as simple as picking up a customer demands forethought—verifying the flight number and where she is expecting to meet you, getting her cell phone number in case of complications, making sure your car is clean, and monitoring the arrival time of the flight as the time draws near. That's simple, isn't it? Deceptively so, or there would be fewer people stranded at the airport delayed, frustrated, or even angry that a few simple things had not been accounted for and anticipated.

CRITICAL SUCCESS FACTOR 4: DEPENDABILITY

I mentioned earlier that our pilot assumed the role of president of DaveAir. He took ownership of the airplane, the flight plan, a backup landing site, and our overall safety. You need to act like you are the president for whatever you're responsible. Learn to think like an owner. Even in an entry-level position, you can become the "head" of your assigned responsibility—be the president of the mailroom if that's your domain. A well-known speaker asks his listeners, "When's the last time you changed the oil in your rental car?" You act differently when you are the owner. There's an accountability and dependability associated with ownership. Owners have a finish-line mentality, and they follow through to completion. They focus on the vital details.

> *There are two kinds of people, those who do the work and those who take the credit. Try to be in the first group; there is less competition there.*
> —INDIRA GANDHI (1917–1984), PRIME MINISTER OF INDIA

When our boys were younger, their grandfather often told them a parable:

For want of a nail, the shoe was lost,
For want of the shoe, the horse was lost,
For want of the horse, the rider was lost,
For want of the rider, the battle was lost,
For want of the battle, the kingdom was lost,
And all for the want of a horseshoe nail![3]

While a little hokey, the parable makes an incredibly important point about taking care of the "vital few"—being dependable in areas that matter. William's eyes may have glazed over when he was ten, but now as a young naval officer operating a nuclear-powered submarine, he gets the point. Follow-through is critically important, no matter what our jobs.

Even if your organization doesn't promote the idea of ownership, you can develop it on your own. What is the best indication of ownership? Dependability—it's part of an owner's DNA, because any undertaking would fail without it. I once conducted a study to discover what characteristics senior managers most valued in younger associates. Far and away, *dependability* was clearly what senior managers valued most in their employees.

I encourage client organizations to intentionally create "ownership cultures." Fostering an environment in which employees "own" the company's mission, strategy, and goals profoundly affects productivity—even more so when employees own their jobs and accept responsibility for making the organization successful. The opening quote from the movie *Office Space* illustrates how ineffective some companies can be at creating this feeling among its staff. I honestly believe that most employees want to excel at their jobs and want their organizations to prosper, but management sometimes makes this kind of emotional ownership difficult. As a result, some companies' workers do as little real work as possible as depicted in *Office Space*.

Dependable individuals plan, organize, and finish their projects. They follow through—you can rely on them to get things done. They are purposeful, determined, and have very high standards. They regularly communicate essential information about the status of a project or customer order, explaining what still needs to be done, by whom, and when. When they blend their initiative and dependability with humor and good interpersonal relationships, they are powerhouses of productivity, and that is why customers and senior managers love them.

A few years ago, I participated in a talent review session during which a CEO and several of her key leaders evaluated their high-potential employees to determine the organization's bench strength. When we came to one name on the list, the CEO spoke up and said, "If he had one ounce of dependability, he'd be dangerous." Everyone at the table laughed because they knew immediately what she meant. The guy was brilliant and well-liked. Despite his talent, this high-potential employee had a major derailer. He lacked dependability—he didn't plan, wasn't organized, and didn't follow through. According to the talent review team, his coordination with other executives was terrible. He relied too heavily on his creative genius. None of the other executives felt that he could handle the senior job in his division. Then, the moment of truth . . . the CEO turned to me and asked, "Can he be fixed?" After a few seconds, I said, "Yes . . . if he is given a compelling reason to change." I went on to explain that it was time for someone to tell him the truth. His eccentricities were not funny anymore. He had to change dramatically over the next couple of years, or he'd be toast.

CRITICAL SUCCESS FACTOR 5: RESOURCEFULNESS

Organizations desperately want resourceful employees—the fifth CSF. Individuals with this critical skill always seem to find a way to solve problems and to get the job done.

When we're resourceful, we solve problems and deal effectively with difficult situations. We accept responsibility to understand the nature of the problem and what is needed to resolve it. The resourceful person uses imagination and inventiveness to marshal assets to reach an important goal. This person may have exactly the same resources as another but uses them more skillfully in the accomplishment of a critical task. A manager finds it incredibly refreshing when an employee discovers a problem and then exercises initiative to address that problem in a capable way before the manager even knows about it.

A Primer on How to Become Resourceful

1. Seek out challenging assignments at work.
2. Spend time with people who challenge you to be resourceful and to pursue excellence.
3. Acquire a mentor who asks you tough questions about how you're doing in your job.
4. Develop three solutions for a specific problem that needs solving and describe the pros and cons for each approach.
5. Find a way to break a big task into small, more achievable tasks, and then create a plan and sequence to complete them.

Many times I have met with senior executives who close their office doors and then give me an uncensored view of their team. In one such meeting, my client expressed tremendous frustration with a particular individual because she "always had to do his thinking for him." My client's frustration stemmed from her team member's failure to analyze a problem and to identify multiple options for handling it before bringing it to her. His frequent pattern involved bringing a problem to his boss without applying his own resourcefulness to solve it in advance. My client often felt her staff member was trying to delegate the problem to her—"to take the monkey off his back and to put it on mine." At one point in the fairly animated conversation, she exclaimed, "What am I paying him for?" She wanted him to be resourceful and to solve the problem without her if possible. If he was not able to solve it without her authority, he should at least come to her with an understanding of the root causes, the implications of the problem on employees or customers, the options for handling the problem, and a carefully thought-out recommendation for the best option.

"Houston, we have a problem" is the unforgettable line in one of my favorite movies, *Apollo 13*. Even though we know the ending before the movie starts, it's a great story about resourcefulness. Although we think of the astronauts as the heroes, the real supermen in the Apollo 13 saga are the engineers on the ground. They have to figure out how to fix the highly sophisticated and complex air filtration system with available materials in the lunar module 165,000 miles from Earth. The crisis requires tremendous imagination and inventiveness. Ed Smylie and his fellow ingenious engineers end up saving the day with cardboard, duct tape, and a plastic bag. The Apollo 13 astronauts owe their very lives to Smylie and his team. When we apply resourcefulness to complex problems, we earn the undying loyalty of those we help.

There will always be problems, as Murphy's Law predicts. Customers change their minds at the last minute, machinery breaks down, and bad weather creates havoc. Being resourceful means we step up and find an innovative way around these obstacles. We take the initiative and use our wits and creativity to create new solutions. Those who fail in such situations usually see the unexpected problem as an excuse rather than a call to greater levels of initiative, effort, and creativity.

A young woman told me recently that she intended to leave her company. When I asked why, she said that she wasn't growing there and didn't see much of an opportunity in the future. I knew she was on the high-potential list, so I encouraged her to let a member of senior management know of her dissatisfaction. The company stood to lose one of its best performers, yet I couldn't blame her for wanting to keep growing. We often can't control what assignments are given to us, but one reason she was so good was that she intentionally sought out challenging assignments that would develop her strengths.

This excellent employee knew that in order to reach her potential, she had to keep growing in her resourcefulness. She sought out opportunities at work that would get her out of her comfort zone. Six months later she left for a competitor who had a reputation for developing its employees.

Some of my clients call employees who don't contribute significantly to the company "Gentlemen Cs." They don't offend people or make waves; they just hide in nondescript jobs and try to stay safely in their comfort zone. These C-level performers are not bad enough to fire, but they're not really excelling at their work. They're not growing in their resourcefulness, and at some point, they just become dead weight to the organization.

When I survey successful members of organizations about what most contributed to their development, no one ever responds with "a management seminar." While I strongly believe in the value of management training to acquire important information, we tend to grow the most when we're out of our comfort zones—such as stretch assignments that demand high levels of resourcefulness. Such situations may demand skills that we do not have, put us into unfamiliar territory with new rules for success, or stress our mental or physical capacities nearly to the breaking point.

I often recommend that corporate leaders assign a high-potential employee to a business turnaround or a start-up as a major developmental opportunity. A challenging assignment during which we get feedback and see results often leads to tremendous growth.

If we want to become more resourceful, then we should pay attention to the people with whom we spend time. We tend to become like the people we hang out with. There is a water table effect in play with respect to the people we're around. Our water level is unlikely to rise higher than those in our midst. We may like our friends and enjoy being with them, but we should also have an honest conversation with ourselves to ask if our time with these friends is going to challenge us to become stronger and more resourceful. We should ask ourselves: Do I want to be like them in ten years? Do they push me to pursue excellence? Do I want to emulate their thought processes, skills, and commitment to get the job done?

> *A single conversation across the table with a wise person is better than ten years' mere study of books.*
> —HENRY WADSWORTH LONGFELLOW (1807–1882), AMERICAN POET

We all need a Joe in our lives. Joe was a mentor with whom I had breakfast every month or so when I was younger. He was a savvy, battle-hardened veteran of business, having built, run, and sold several companies. His infectious laugh usually meant, "I've had that problem a dozen times, and I'm still in business—it's likely you will be, too, come tomorrow." He would then help me get perspective on a problem and think of new ways to solve it. The thing I remember most about Joe was that he constantly asked me questions: How did you come to that conclusion? What made you think that was right? What will you do differently next time? Resourceful people are always asking questions of themselves and others. Joe was very hesitant to give solutions and answers, but his questions forced me to discover new ways of looking at an issue and become more resourceful.

CRITICAL SUCCESS FACTOR 6: ABILITY TO LEARN

Columbia Pictures' 1993 movie, *Groundhog Day*, stars Bill Murray as cynical TV weatherman Phil Connors, who covers the famous day on which a groundhog named Punxsutawney Phil determines whether or not spring has arrived. The arrogant, self-centered Connors finds he is compelled to repeat Groundhog Day over and over until he learns some important life lessons. Events repeat themselves day after day, but he keeps missing the point. Over time his cynicism gradually fades, and he learns to love and serve others until he's finally freed from the cycle. Many of us get caught in the same conundrum, not making sense of our experiences or changing our normal patterns to break the cycle. Using wisdom to interpret our circumstances and learn critical lessons about our own effectiveness is a vital skill at work.

To excel at work we must learn continuously and become smarter every day. When we're in school there are valuable skills that are important to master, but the most important skill is to *learn to learn*. Even the sharpest blade gets dull with use; learning is the best tool for sharpening your mind.

Active learning is always preferred to passive learning. To learn actively we have to gather, understand, and apply information rather than letting it act on us. The best sources of new insights are our experiences. We especially need to learn from our successes and failures. We often learn most from our failures and mistakes, so we should plunge headlong into understanding why something didn't go well. T. S. Eliot said, "Some people have the experience and miss the meaning,"[4] just like Phil Connors in *Groundhog Day*.

LEARNING FROM EXPERIENCE

1. Watch the "game films." What worked? What didn't work? What did you learn? What will you do differently next time as a result? What new skill or process could you apply in similar situations?

2. Identify the underlying principles and root causes instead of symptoms and activities. Figure out *why* things worked or didn't work rather than *what* worked or didn't work.

3. Decide if the lessons apply to a broader audience than just yourself. Does this apply to other teams, departments, etc.?

The most important part of learning is doing something with it—applying what we have learned for the next time it is relevant. The ability to transfer learning from one situation to another is called *generalization*. It is the skill that enables us to see past an experience to the broader significance of the event. How can we learn to generalize—to have the experience and *not* miss the meaning?

If there is broader significance, communicate what you have learned. Questions to discover *why* are more important than questions to discover *what*. Seek out root causes. Look around you and be curious. Read a different newspaper than you normally read. Engage with people around you to find out about their lives. Watch documentaries. Befriend the elderly. Take a more senior person in your organization to lunch and ask questions about how his division's strategies support the mission of the organization.

FIRST, PUT GAS IN YOUR PORSCHE

Remember that Critical Success Factors are like a Porsche engine; it can make a Carrera go 170 mph, but it needs high-octane fuel to do so. CSFs must be fueled by passion. Earlier we talked about the attitude of running to win. How many people do we know who are highly talented but content to drift along in life? Talent must be fueled with passion, which stems from a life of purpose and intentionality.

Skilled but passionless people litter the workplace landscape. The Notre Dame football player immortalized in the inspirational film *Rudy* illustrates how even a person with modest skill can excel with passion. At one point the coach berates a more talented player for wasting his talent due to a lackadaisical attitude. The highly talented player slacks off because he feels entitled—"I have a position on this team because I'm so good." To realize his potential he needs Rudy's type of passion.

Passion, however, is *not* a substitute for skill—they are both essential. Rudy only played in one game at Notre Dame because he just didn't have the physical attributes or skill necessary for that level of football, not because he didn't have passion. Some of our colleagues at work are passionate, but their enthusiasm needs to be mixed with CSFs to achieve results.

As one of my favorite stories goes, a man was very good friends with his priest, who happened to be a big boxing fan. The man had tickets to a major heavyweight match and invited the priest. Just before the bell rang, one of the boxers knelt in his corner and passionately made the sign of the cross. Wanting to be respectful of his friend's office, the man said, "Father what does it really mean when the boxer crosses himself?" The priest looked at his friend and laughed, "Son, not much if he can't fight."

A DAUNTING CHALLENGE

The Greek poet Hesiod said in 700 BC, "Badness you can get easily and in quantity. The road is smooth and it lies close by. But in front of excellence [is] sweat, and long and steep is the way to it . . ."[5] The first six Critical Success Factors—self-management, relationship management, forethought, dependability, resourcefulness, and ability to learn—require a lifelong focus of disciplined intentionality. The seventh CSF, the ability to change, describes how we develop and sustain these vital competencies. As with most things in life, going downstream requires so little energy that we're naturally drawn in that direction. Transformation requires that we marshal the resources to go upstream. Not that simple, and not that easy. The payoff is increased effectiveness and the achievement of success and significance, regardless of what type of work we do.

11

Run Your
Best Race

It is important to remember that we cannot become
what we need to be by remaining what we are.
—Max DePree, Chairman Emeritus, Herman Miller, Inc.

Acrisis transformed my son's life during an essential rite of passage. Trying out for a youth sports team or any competitive activity is a defining moment in a child's life. Jim tried out for a Little League baseball team when he turned eleven. Making the eleven and twelve-year-old team is a big deal, but *not* making it is a bigger deal. Most of the boys who try out make the cut, but a few don't—Jim didn't. Why not? The simple answer is that he didn't do well in the tryouts. The underlying reason was that I didn't help him prepare. The tryouts are always in the middle of February, which is a miserable time to do anything outdoors. What I later learned was that many of the parents started working with their boys in December. They fielded grounders, threw to first base, caught long fly balls, and went to the batting cage—all the skills that would be tested in the tryouts. Getting ready for tryouts wasn't rocket science—it just took time and focus from both of us. I didn't help Jim get ready for the tryouts as many of the other dads had done.

It breaks the heart of a parent to see his child's heart broken. Anne and I grieved for Jim as a cloud hung over his young life. It was a crisis for our whole family, but Jim had to go to school the next day and face the derision of his peers. Most boys who didn't make the eleven and twelve-year-old team just dropped out of baseball. So to add injury to insult, Jim was assigned to a younger team where he would be playing with a bunch of ten-year-olds. Understandably he wanted to quit, but we gently reminded him of our long-standing agreement that when he started something, he needed to see it through.

The night the teams were announced, Coach Arnold, the coach of the younger team, called to speak to Jim. "Jim, I want you to be my starting pitcher, and you are going to help us win the league championship this year." It was obvious that only one answer would be accepted. "Yes, sir." The affirmation continued the next night at the parent's meeting. To the parents and the other players, Coach Arnold said, "Through a fluke in the draft this year, we got Jim on our team. He will be our starting pitcher, and he's going to help us win the league championship."

Coach Arnold is held at a level barely below sainthood in our family. He intuitively knew what not making the older team meant to Jim, and he determined to transform a young boy's crisis into character.

Coach Arnold worked on Jim's pitching, and his message was consistent. "You have great natural talent, but to realize your potential is going to require work and discipline. I expect no less than total focus and attention when you're on the mound." He also worked on Jim's attitude. He was one of those kids who was born happy; and when he entered grade school, it was a shock to his system that some kids were cynical and mean. The inevitable tough interactions with some of those kids eroded his self-confidence. You could almost hear Jim changing his self-talk: "Coach Arnold believes in me, and the team is depending on me. I have to toughen up and not let the jerks get to me anymore."

It was a great season and the team did well. Jim gave his team the league's limit of six solid innings of pitching every week. Everything went swimmingly until the team's biggest game of the year—the first round of the league championship series. Jim pitched two scoreless innings. In the third, the wheels fell off the wagon. Two outs, still scoreless, he walked three straight hitters with the other team's best hitter now at bat. Anne and I did what any normal, supportive parents would do: we prayed for Coach Arnold to take him out!

Obviously, Jim's anxiety about the game threatened to overwhelm his ability to pitch, so the coach called time and walked to the mound. "Jim, I need you to get another out, and I need you focused and in the game. You've gotten this kid out before, and you're going to do it again." Coach Arnold smiled, squeezed his shoulder, and walked back to the dugout. Four pitches later, the batter struck out. And yes, several weeks later the team went on to win the league championship as Coach Arnold predicted. The following year, Jim made the eleven and twelve-year-old team and went on to a great season as a pitcher and first baseman. His year on Coach Arnold's team laid the groundwork for playing on a highly competitive varsity baseball team in high school and later becoming a three-year starter on his college football team.

THE REUNION

Even the most self-assured among us entertain private doubts. When we hit adversity, we wonder if we can bounce back. This book provides a daunting list of personal attributes—the distilled essence of what separates the successful from those who derail. If we cannot develop these qualities, are we relegated to the ranks of the working disenchanted for the rest of our lives? Are we doomed to be nothing more than the sum total of what we are now?

Have you been to your high school reunion lately? It's always interesting to see how our old classmates have fared. Some are unrecognizable—they have a lot less hair. Gravity has changed their faces, and too much food and not enough exercise have changed their shapes. Many are on their second or even third marriage and have several children. It's striking how some seem frozen in their adolescent mind-set. Our good friend, Joe, is just like he was in high school—even his inflections and mannerisms are the same.

Are we doomed to be nothing more than the sum total of what we are now?

Most of us graduated from high school with dreams and ambitions. Maybe we wanted to get out of our hometown, do better than our parents, or have a meaningful career. The longer we talk with some old classmates, the more we see in their faces that the initial bravado of "everything's fantastic" diminishes. We see in their countenance that their dreams of youth have faded like an old yearbook photograph. They left high school to face a challenging and uncertain world, ill-equipped to become the person they really wanted to be.

THE GRAVITATIONAL PULL OF THE FAMILIAR

Why don't people realize their dreams? Why have so few, even the ones with talent, achieved their ambitions? Most never achieved enough escape velocity to get beyond the gravitational pull of their comfort zone—a space that requires little risk and none of the self-discipline it takes to grow and to be different.

More than 850 men, women, and children died when the giant ferry, *MS Estonia*, sank in the Baltic Sea during a 1993 storm. Many of those who tragically perished clung to the outside railings of the huge white ship as it sank, pulling them under the frigid water to their deaths. A bitter irony frustrated the rescuers—dozens of empty life boats bobbed on the ocean waves, just a few feet away from the victims clinging to the "safety railing." Many simply wouldn't let go of the boat—the familiar. No doubt the howling wind, the crashing waves, the frigid water, the piercing darkness, and the screams of the dying paralyzed many into a state of inaction. Perhaps we would have clung to the railings like so many others. Comfort zones hold us captive even when they're not really that comfortable or safe. They're just familiar. Our "boat" at work may be taking on water, but at least it's a boat we know.

In some cases, our familiar strength becomes a weakness when we depend on it too heavily. A general counsel of a large company was promoted to a senior line management position. Darlene previously managed a handful of attorneys but now had five senior department heads reporting to her. Her boss received so many complaints about her management style that he seriously questioned his decision to promote her. Self-control and disciplined toughness helped her succeed in law school and in her early career, but now her rigid, high-control style rankled the experienced executives who reported to her. These new direct reports were mature, strategic, and successful in their own right—they needed very little management from anyone. During an especially candid moment, Darlene admitted that she was *afraid of losing control.* She clung to the secure and familiar safety railing of control—but her

> *Change by its very nature tends to upset our personal balance and make everything more stressful, so we avoid it. A comfort zone insulates us from the tension and uncertainty of personal transformation.*

career threatened to sink unless she let go. Her lifeboat was to develop a supportive, empowering management style to rebuild the trust of her direct reports—a change that required intense personal change.

Change by its very nature tends to upset our personal balance and make everything more stressful, so we avoid it. A comfort zone insulates us from the tension and uncertainty of personal transformation. A young man with a degree in business from a prestigious northeastern university originally intended to interview with some leading companies, but after graduation, he ended up working in a part-time job on his university campus that was not just a dead end, but it was a sinkhole. When asked why he didn't try to move on, he smiled and said, "I'm too comfortable." His job and income fell far below his potential, but it was easy money, and he made enough to pay his bills. His womb of comfort outmatched his boredom and desire for a more challenging job.

More change in the world of work occurred in the last twenty years than any period in history. Technology, globalization, and telecommunication are changing the way we live and work; however, the most important transformation must still occur *in us*—the abilities to learn and to change rapidly are now basic requirements for effectiveness in the workplace.

> *The key to transformation is in understanding and then harnessing the forces at play in our lives.*

Why are New Year's resolutions so transient? Why is it that some people seem to make change happen while most don't? Personal transformation is the most difficult challenge in life. Some people seem to adopt personal change and become different. They lose weight and keep it off. They raise their EQ. They take purposeful steps to increase their technical skills. For others, change remains a pipe dream. It's imagined but never realized. How do successful individuals make change happen? The seventh Critical Success Factor is personal transformation, the *ability to change* ourselves.

The key to transformation is in understanding and then harnessing the forces at play in our lives. We typically experience some forces pushing toward change while other forces resist change. It is critical that we understand these forces and learn to use them. It is also essential that we understand what it takes to sustain a change. Change typically starts with an eye-opening emotional contradiction that gets our attention.

CRITICAL SUCCESS FACTOR 7: ABILITY TO CHANGE

At age eleven most things came easily for my son Jim, so it was a shock when he didn't make the baseball team; it represented a huge contradiction in his young life. It was the first big thing that didn't go his way, so it prompted him to wonder why it didn't work out in the way he expected. The event woke him up emotionally, as incidents that promote change usually do.

A *transformational event* is a wake-up call that can lead to personal change. We see this in a number of life circumstances. For example, when we look in the mirror and don't like what we see, if the contradiction is strong enough it becomes a catalyst to think about losing weight, getting a haircut, or other resolutions. It does not bring about change, but the contradiction prompts us to react: mentally, emotionally, physically, or spiritually. The contradiction jars us and unfreezes our perceptions, at least for a moment.

Many organizations utilize multi-rater questionnaires to develop their employees. This 360-degree feedback typically asks a person's manager, peers, and others to rate him on a variety of competencies. A report summarizes his performance and is particularly effective at identifying blind spots. Because the feedback is anonymous, raters are usually quite candid. The results of this feedback are often contradictory, eye-opening, and catalytic. A colleague's client reacted so strongly to his 360-degree report that he overturned a table and stormed out of the room. He and his raters had strikingly different perceptions of his effectiveness.

When we experience this wake-up call, we react in one of two ways. We either *affirm* the information by reflection and possible action, or we *deny* that it's true. Affirmation lets us thoughtfully consider the feedback we've received, while denial insulates us and deflects the feedback away from us. We claim to be misunderstood and the victim of misperceptions—"I'm really not that way," "I've changed," "No one understands me," or "I have a terrible manager." This stage is truly the moment of truth, because at this point we either lapse back into our comfort zone of familiarity or we decide to take the next step of change.

If we accept feedback from our manager, a 360-degree exercise, or other sources, we can consider what changes to make and how to make them. When we don't accept feedback, we deny ourselves the potential benefits of personal transformation.

THE COMPELLING WHYS

The emotional contradiction or transformational event slows us down enough to consider changing, but *compelling whys* are what actually drive us to change. Compelling whys fall into three categories:

1. *Pain* is the most unpleasant but the strongest driver of change. When we receive negative performance feedback or we're passed over for a promotion or raise, it creates pain. Used effectively, pain can drive us to address issues in our work performance.

2. *Potential consequences* are probable sources of pain, but the prospect of that pain is so unpleasant that it can change our behavior. Many actions are prompted by consequences: for example, when your boss tells you that if you're late again, you'll be fired.

3. *Future promise* shows the benefits of change. If we lose weight, we'll look and feel better. If we work hard and reach our goals, we'll be promoted and earn more money.

When I'm asked to coach a leader who has serious deficiencies in his or her behavior at work, I usually ask the sponsor of the coaching engagement to describe the forces supporting and opposing change in that person's life. I especially want to know which compelling reasons will drive the person to grow: for example, will he lose his job if he doesn't change?

I recently worked with a manager who was a brilliant technical engineer but interpersonally abusive. The plant was having terrible retention problems because his direct reports couldn't stand working with this harsh, stubborn micromanager. His boss hesitated to define any consequences for the manager if he failed to improve, because the board liked the results the manager consistently achieved. I predicted a low probability of success because of the absence of any compelling whys. A simple appeal to the manager's goodwill was not enough to motivate the considerable changes that the plant manager needed to make.

In the movie *Remember the Titans,* Denzel Washington plays Herman Boone, the head football coach of a Virginia high school that becomes racially integrated for the first time over the summer vacation. In a moving scene during preseason practice, Coach Boone makes his players run to a battleground near Gettysburg where he describes the history surrounding the famous battle:

This green field right here, painted red, bubblin' with the blood of young boys. Smoke and hot lead pouring right through their bodies. Listen to their souls, men. I killed my brother with malice in my heart. Hatred destroyed my family. You listen, and you take a lesson from the dead. If we don't come together right now on this hallowed ground, we, too, will be destroyed, just like they were. I don't care if you like each other or not, but you will respect each other. And maybe . . . I don't know, maybe we'll learn to play this game like men.[1]

Coach Boone uses all three compelling whys with his young players. In the early weeks of practice, they constantly fight with each other along racial lines—the *pain* of alienation. He reminds them that if they don't come together and cross the racial divide, they "will be destroyed," both as a team and as individuals—the *consequences*. He also holds out the *future promise* throughout the season that they can win the state football championship.

THE INEVITABLE OPPOSING FORCES

Most attempts at change meet powerful forces resisting our new direction. For example, what if our boss is critical and toxic, which negatively impacts our job performance and even our overall life outlook and self-esteem? Quitting that job makes perfect sense until we acknowledge the set of forces in opposition. A significant pay cut or a much longer commute puts formidable obstacles in our way and may make quitting seem impossible.

Sometimes the most daunting obstacles are of our own making. A young woman who worked as a filing clerk in a huge medical practice hated her job but had very few career options due to her limited education. She wanted to return to school, but there were a number of barriers in the way that made it difficult to fulfill this goal. Most notably, she had a problem with alcohol and was in a very dysfunctional relationship. She and her boyfriend would go out drinking after work almost every night, where they hung out with a group of friends who also hated their jobs. The third and most powerful force was that her great uncle had actually won a lottery and left her a small trust fund. She was not wealthy, but she used the quarterly checks from the trust fund to insulate herself from the financial pain she would have otherwise experienced with her minimum wage job. It was going to be unbelievably difficult for her to get out of the dead-end canyon she was in, because the barriers to change kept her from moving forward. She reminded me of the indictment in the classic comic strip, *Pogo*: "We have met the enemy, and he is us."[2]

> *There must be compelling reasons for the change that are more powerful than the forces opposing that change; otherwise the change will not occur.*

There must be compelling reasons for the change that are more powerful than the forces opposing that change; otherwise, the change will not occur. We know that we need to seek a more challenging job, to finish college, to overhaul our interpersonal style at work, or start our own business, but the obstacles doom all attempts to change. Our life circumstances may overwhelm any initiative we want to take.

Highly successful people understand the forces for and against change in their lives, and then they either find stronger reasons to change or weaken the forces against change. They employ three key strategies:

1. Find a more compelling reason to move in a new direction. If you have been postponing returning to school, do some research on salaries in the jobs you could get with a degree. The additional money or better job may be enough to move you forward.
2. Weaken the forces against change. If you dread having to repay student loans, then examine the facts. Obstacles often appear more overwhelming than they are. A perceived problem carries as much or more power as a real one. To overcome a perception, we need to get the facts. Find out exactly how much a degree will cost and check out the repayment options. The programs that

loan students money want to make the repayment affordable, so the payments may be more manageable than you thought.

3. Do both of the above. Combining a better reason to change with diminished forces against the change may be the ticket.

Life circumstances can be very frustrating, particularly when they seem out of our control. Some work cultures spawn discouragement and mind-numbing boredom. A job in this type of organization creates a powerful force against change because it depletes the emotional energy we need to move forward. When we lose our excitement about work, we must ask if our commitment can be rekindled. Wisdom guides us to either persevere in the adversity or to move on to a better opportunity.

> *Highly successful people understand the forces for and against change in their lives, and then they either find stronger reasons to change or weaken the forces against change.*

Whether the right answer is to stay in our present job or to move in a new direction, the compelling why must be clear. Psychoanalyst and holocaust survivor Viktor Frankl observed prisoners who survived the Nazi concentration camps and those who did not. Frankl acknowledged that many good things such as health, family, and friends provide meaning in life. But what about in a concentration camp where a person suffers extreme deprivation? He observed that many chose to give up. Almost always, the survivor had a clear *reason* for living. Frankl stated, "He who knows the *why* will be able to bear almost any *how*."[3]

SUSTAINING CHANGE

We all have failed at New Year's resolutions after a few weeks of effort. How do we sustain change? One key is *accountability in a supportive environment*, which explains why programs such as Alcoholics Anonymous and Weight Watchers are often effective. They provide frequent accountability and support from other members who understand the changes being made.

My son, Jim, knew he needed to make fundamental changes in his attitude, focus, and effort, but Coach Arnold's consistent accountability and support made the difference and enabled him to put the changes into action. He also had ample opportunities to apply the new behaviors during the season. This is why a management coach or mentor in a work setting can be very helpful. A coach can provide accountability and help as we develop a new set of work behaviors. When we know someone is truly in our corner, we can sincerely hear just about any feedback they give.

If you don't have a mentor, you may want to find one. Look for someone who's more experienced, has integrity, and is well-regarded in your organization—someone whom you would really like to emulate. It doesn't need to be formal. Try taking a person you respect to breakfast a few times to ask for his or her advice on how to handle some of the challenges you are facing. Ask how she navigated her career to get to where she is now. If the person's advice is helpful and you enjoy your time together, continue to meet with her. The right mentor will gladly help you and will find it satisfying to help another member of the organization.

Some who succeed at personal change enlist the help of a "Board of Change." While it's always tempting to poll our friends, successful individuals often meet regularly with several people from different walks of life, ages, or backgrounds. The key is to find individuals with greater maturity and a broader perspective. Friends at work tend to agree with you ("Yeah, she's just a terrible manager") while a mentor may help you see that people who learn to thrive under that "terrible manager" almost always get promoted. When successful people have an important decision, they routinely talk with their "board members" to get wise counsel. The right answer often reflects a hybrid of opinions and insights.

If you feel reluctant or embarrassed to ask an older, more experienced person for advice, that's very understandable. Keep in mind that most people are flattered to be asked and value the opportunity to share what they've learned. Getting sound counsel starts with asking.

The illustration at the end of this chapter summarizes the major steps in personal change. A graphically enhanced, full color version of this model is available for free at runwiththebulls.net. It can be downloaded for wallpaper or as a poster.

CONFORMING VERSUS TRANSFORMING

For many, change is really about *conforming* to the behavior that most people deem normal. Conformity often results from pressure by peers, bosses, or even the culture at work. We want to fit in, so we conform to someone else's expectations. Change brought about by conforming remains superficial because it's change only on the outside. It's like putting a new coat of paint on an old car; it's only cosmetic.

> *Change brought about by conforming remains superficial because it's change only on the outside. It's like putting a new coat of paint on an old car; it's only cosmetic.*

Conforming to others' expectations creates some temporary relief because it takes the pressure off. It also leaves us feeling empty because conformity is always the enemy of significance. Conformity goes downstream, while significance goes upstream—this is why so few people choose significance. Those around us expect us to go downstream with them, and we don't like going against the pressure of others' approval. We feel anxious being separated from the pack.

Substantive change is about *transformation*, a change of form or nature. A sculptor changes clay into an object of art. Transformation requires radical alteration—it changes who we are.

A hydroelectric dam is an amazing combination of the physical power of the water stored above the dam and the technology of huge turbines generating electricity. The water above the dam is called *potential energy.* Water passing through the turbines to create electricity is called *kinetic energy.* The turbines transform water pressure into energy; passive potential becomes active power. This transformational process takes only one step by the dam operator—the opening of the control gate to send the water through the turbines. Your first step in transforming your mind and character is to open the emotional "control gate." Then you must marshal the forces that are driving the change to move forward.

> *Your first step in transforming your mind and character is to open the emotional "control gate." Then you must marshal the forces that are driving the change to move forward.*

A GREAT ADVENTURE

We live in a world filled with challenge and uncertainty. We run with the bulls every day, and that's unlikely to change. What we can change is *how* we run the race, and that's what this book is about.

Helen Keller said that "life is either a great adventure, or it's nothing at all."[4] My hope is that every day you will find significance in your work and that you will discover a grand adventure. A life dedicated to the pursuit of high and noble ends is not an easy life, but it is filled with adventure and fulfillment that cannot be experienced any other way. Given the huge role that work plays in our lives, my hope is that in the end you'll feel that you invested those years well, and when you go to bed at night, you'll never wonder why you are on the planet.

Note to reader: To help you apply these ideas in a practical way as you work on real changes in your own life, go to runwiththebulls.net to complete exercises for the six primary steps of change.

Summary of Section 3

EXCEPTIONAL COMPETENCE

The preceding four chapters described the seven Critical Success Factors that make us truly competent regardless of the work that we do. Despite personal brilliance and a vast array of technical skills, we will fail to perform effectively in our jobs without these seven CSFs—self-management, relationship management, forethought, dependability, resourcefulness, an ability to learn, and an ability to change. Effectiveness in these seven attributes leads to exceptional competence.

To run with the bulls without getting trampled, run with exceptional competence!

EPILOGUE

A sphere of mystery exists whenever we are dealing with things
that are finally unpredictable, where whatever order exists cannot
be understood well enough to give us the control we desire.[1]
—LARRY CRABB, PH.D., PSYCHOLOGIST AND AUTHOR

The first thing I intended to buy with the money I earned from my job as a shoe salesman was a sound system—the cutting edge of new audio technology called "quadraphonic sound." I knew I'd never make enough money to buy a new "quad," so I saved for a kit that required assembly.

I worked and saved for months, first buying a speaker, then three others, an amplifier, and other components. In the meantime I soldered away, connecting wires, transistors, capacitors, and switches.

After what seemed like an interminable period of time, the gleaming new system was complete. A speaker was positioned in each of the four corners of my bedroom, and the amplifier was wired and ready. I wanted my dad to be the first to hear my new sound system, so I readied an album and invited him up to my room.

In the opening seconds of the album's first cut, it became apparent that no finer sound had ever been reproduced in the history of mankind. The most discriminating and demanding audiophile in the world would have surely attested that this system, for years to come, would set the standard for excellence. The purity of sound, the crispness of the notes, and the authentic reproduction of the artist were truly remarkable. The many months of hard work—dealing with people's smelly feet, customers who had to try on a hundred pairs of shoes to get the right ones, and the burns from the soldering gun had all come down to this. And it was worth it!

Unbeknownst to me, a late afternoon thunderstorm had just rolled into our neighborhood. About fifteen seconds into the first song, a gigantic lightning bolt struck the tree outside my bedroom window. Gazillions of volts of electricity jumped from the tree across to the wiring of our home and went straight into my new sound system. It literally went up in smoke.

After opening the windows in my room to clear the smoke, I began to grasp the magnitude of what had just happened—all of my savings, the untold hours of work at my job and in building the kit—gone in an instant. It was a foundational moment in my young life. In the weeks that followed, I looked at the charred elements of my sound system on the floor of my room and grieved life's injustices.

Getting out of my funk involved a number of challenges. First was not to give in to the natural tendency to feel like a hopeless victim of fate. The next challenge was to accept that the hard work and my goal were worthwhile despite my disappointment. I had to start over with the newfound wisdom and humility that only adversity can instill in us.

Life's lightning strikes with haphazard fury and blows the circuits of our best-laid plans. These events can feed the darkly pessimistic perception that our lives are careening randomly out of control. As Larry

Crabb stated in the opening quote, none of us really have the level of "control we desire."

Lightning also strikes in the workplace. We go to work with the belief that our jobs have meaning, direction, and control, yet events and decisions in the workplace are often unpredictable and far beyond our influence.

The world of work is chaotic for many, and constant change creates turbulence and uncertainty. It's easy to recoil emotionally, lose perspective, and become the victim of a terrible boss or a plant closing. Our personal hopes and dreams begin to flounder.

Earlier I stated that we run with the bulls whether we want to or not. It becomes especially dangerous when we think the organization's bulls are out to get us *personally,* because we get defensive and feel victimized. We need to remember that these bulls are indifferent to our hopes and dreams. Circumstances at work are not unfair—they're indifferent. The energy we waste personalizing those circumstances diminishes the resourcefulness we need to get out of the bulls' way and to get to whatever arena we aspire to reach.

Run With the Bulls Without Getting Trampled endorses the belief that working skillfully helps us stay out of harm's way and thrive at work. Many people who direct their work lives toward meaningful ends and who make a difference in the workplace often possess many of the following attributes:

1. These individuals know they are in a race, and they are running to win. They possess a *thoughtful commitment* to and seriousness about a life of significance. They created careers that support significance by choosing jobs with certain characteristics:

   • Inspires passion
   • Fits who we are

- Serves others
- Provides meaning

Their thoughtful commitments make them highly intentional people, as evidenced by:

- Strategic mind-set
- Disciplined preparation
- Commitment to action
- Courage in the face of difficulty

2. Their *authentic character* is distinguished in three ways:

- Trustworthiness
- Persistence
- Avoidance of the derailment factors

3. They possess *seven Critical Success Factors* that became the foundation of their *exceptional competence* at work:

- Self-management
- Effective interpersonal relationships
- Forethought
- Dependability
- Resourcefulness
- Ability to learn
- Ability to change

This very powerful combination of thoughtful commitment, authentic character, and exceptional competence inevitably results in: *confident humility* and *extraordinary performance.*

> *Thoughtful Commitment*
>
> +
>
> *Authentic Character*
>
> +
>
> *Exceptional Competence*
>
> =
>
> *Confident Humility and Extraordinary Performance*

WHAT SHOULD I DO?

It all starts with the fundamental decision to pursue a life of purpose and significance and to manifest this commitment in your work. Our life destination determines who we become, because we're transformed into the person our aspirations require. If you're aiming low, you don't need to become much. If you're aiming high, the attributes listed above need to be your waking obsession.

Our life destination determines who we become, because we're transformed into the person our aspirations require.

What I am proposing is neither simple nor easy, but it does offer the significance and meaning for which many of us yearn. The opening line from Scott Peck's classic, *The Road Less Traveled*, states with startling simplicity, "Life is difficult."[2] Sustaining *commitment*, *character*, and *competence* in your work will undoubtedly be one of the most difficult challenges of your life. If it was simple or easy, many people would do it. Overwhelmed by formidable obstacles, some will never even leave the starting gate to enter this great race of life—to work with significance and purpose.

Many feel limited by their backgrounds or by decisions made earlier in life, and the development of the attributes described throughout this book seems impossible. I would never diminish the limitations and challenges you face. What I will point out is that most extraordinary accomplishments are achieved by very ordinary people who face the same struggles you and I do, yet they chose to pursue a life of significance and made the hard decisions required to circumvent a life of mediocrity.

A PERSONAL NOTE

We are all writing the story of our lives, and I am presently writing a new chapter in my own life story. I frequently ask myself what I need to do differently going forward. My life is filled with uncertainty as I contemplate a departure from the career into which I have poured my life energies over the last twenty years.

Peter Drucker, the most brilliant organizational theorist of the modern era, foresaw much of the organizational change we've experienced over the last four to five decades and predicted that organizational change at an accelerating pace would remain a sure constant in the world of work. Drucker believed strongly that organizations (and people) must "stop pouring resources into things that have already achieved their purpose."[3] As I compose this new life chapter, I'm trying to figure out which of my efforts have achieved their purpose, what may be holding me back, and what I must stop pouring resources into. What work should I stop doing? Which opportunities should I turn down? I have anxious moments and find it very difficult to let go of the safety rails of the familiar. Although I find change to be unsettling, it also holds great promise.

How I invest my life is of paramount importance because I believe that a personal and loving God created me for a purpose. His purpose for my life creates an accountability to do something more than just trying to fill my days with self-fulfillment. My faith also fills the gap between life's occasional randomness and the control I desire but often cannot find.

Drucker's words remind me of what one of the authors of the New Testament urged: ". . . let us strip off anything that slows us down or holds us back . . . and let us run with patience the particular race that God has set before us."[4] I believe that regardless of our spiritual perspective, our backgrounds, or our present circumstances, we should aim high, live with purpose, be courageous, let go of whatever is holding us back, and then, run to win!

In *The Chronicles of Narnia*, C. S. Lewis depicts the classic battle between good and evil. In volume seven, *The Last Battle*, all hope appears lost. One of the main characters, Tirian, sees his fellow warriors go down, and as his own death appears near, he makes a profound statement about his life purpose. "His only thought now was to sell his life as dearly as he could."[5]

Whatever amount of time that I've been given *to work* cries out to be used well . . . to be significant; and at the end, I want to sell my life as dearly as I can.

INTRODUCTION TO ONLINE ASSESSMENT AND DEVELOPMENTAL RESOURCES

The greatest of all faults, I should say, is to be conscious of none.
—THOMAS CARLYLE (1795–1881),
SCOTTISH ESSAYIST, SATIRIST, AND HISTORIAN

R*un with the Bulls Without Getting Trampled* is based upon my interviews with thousands of leaders and individual contributors. Many were highly successful in their respective organizations, while others struggled in their jobs for a variety of reasons. My study of these individuals identified the qualities that made them successful, and the preceding chapters provide you the distilled essence of those characteristics. While experts never fully agree, a fairly broad consensus exists as to what attributes make people effective in their chosen work. My conclusions are generally consistent with the findings of others who have studied what makes individuals succeed or derail in the workplace.

The good news is that the qualities described in this book can be developed. Through focused attention and disciplined effort, we can grow in our capabilities. The purpose of the online assessments and developmental resources is twofold—first, to *assess* your level of mastery of each of these vital qualities presented throughout the book; and second, to suggest a few ideas that may help you *develop* these characteristics more fully.

To help you determine your own level of mastery of these important characteristics, I have provided a number of self-assessments that you may use to target personal attributes you want to improve upon while noting your strengths and potential derailers as well. These computer-scored tests and developmental tools are available at **runwiththebulls.net**.

ACCURATE DEPICTIONS OF WHO WE REALLY ARE

Self-awareness is one of the qualities that almost always characterizes highly successful individuals. Obviously, tools of this nature reflect an individual's level of self-awareness and are somewhat subjective. The value of this type of exercise is a greater understanding of the quality, which can lead to our focused efforts to grow in a particular dimension.

> *Honest criticism is hard to take, particularly from a relative, a friend, an acquaintance, or a stranger.*
> —FRANKLIN P. JONES (1887–1929), AMERICAN BUSINESSMAN

Feedback from others provides external validation and often breaks through our defenses, self-denial, and rationalization that prevent us from having an accurate picture of our strengths and weaknesses. After taking the online assessment, share your results with someone who knows you well such as a colleague at work, a boss, a good friend, or a spouse. When asking others for feedback, share with

them the importance of their
feedback and encourage them
to be candid. As to your part,
prepare yourself to be open to
new insights—some positive,
some not so positive—and the

> *Would to God that I could see*
> *myself as others do.*
> —Robert Burns (1759–1796),
> Scottish poet

opportunities for growth that are presented to you through this valuable
feedback. Be prepared to feel defensive, but be *more* prepared to learn
from whomever you ask for feedback.

WHY SHOULD I DO THIS?

Earlier in the book, I discussed the term *aboutism*, which explains why
many people never get off dead center in their lives and work. They have
great-sounding intentions and talk "about" what they want to accomplish. A signal that someone is probably not all that serious is the use of
the word *should*. "I really should go back to school." It's not all that believable. Contrast the previous statement with, "I am going back to school
next fall. I'm scheduled to take the SAT on December 12. My application
for admission will be mailed on Monday morning. I've assembled all the
information for the financial aid packet." This set of statements is more
believable because the person is going on the offense. He is taking action.
There are plans with specific dates attached.

Run With the Bulls Without Getting Trampled represents a clarion call to
action. The online resources provide you with a practical assessment to
help you gauge in what dimensions you need to grow and then recommend developmental steps to turn awareness into action. The planning

guide takes you through the steps needed to develop the vital qualities required to succeed in any endeavor.

I urge you in the strongest of terms to now go on the offense— move forward with purpose and intentionality. Just go to the Web site (runwiththebulls.net) shown below and begin your great adventure.

Notes

Chapter One

1. Ernest Hemingway, *The Sun Also Rises* (New York: Simon & Schuster, Inc., 1995).
2. Gary Gray, *Running with the Bulls, Fiestas, Corridas, Toreros, and an American's Adventure in Pamplona* (Guilford, CT: The Lyons Press, 2001).
3. Hemingway, Ibid.

Chapter Two

1. elise.com, s.v. George Bernard Shaw, *A Splendid Torch*, http://www.elise.com /quotes/a/george_bernard_shaw_a_splendid_torch.php.
2. Lev Grossman, "Grow Up? Not So Fast," *Time*, January 24, 2005, p. 52.
3. Lewis Carroll, *Alice's Adventures in Wonderland*, 1865.
4. Clay Graham (screenwriter), *The Drew Carey Show*, "In Ramada Da Vida," episode 76, season 4, aired September 30, 1998.
5. Gregg Easterbrook, "The New Science of Happiness," *Time*, January 17, 2005.
6. Richard Friedenberg (screenwriter), *A River Runs Through It* (Sony Pictures, 1992).
7. John Grisham, *The Broker* (New York: Doubleday, 2005).

Chapter Three

1. Ephesians 5:15–16, The Message by Eugene H. Peterson (Colorado Springs: NavPress Publishing Group) Copyright© 1993, 1994, 1995, 1996, 2000, 2001, 2002.

2. Jennifer Crittenden (screenwriter), "The PTA Disbands," *The Simpsons,* episode 124, season 6, aired April, 16, 1995.

3. Eric Lax, *Woody Allen: A Biography,* 2nd edition, revised (Cambridge, MA: Da Capo Press, 2000).

4. Tom Peters, "The Brand Called You," *Fast Company,* August/September 1997.

5. Robert K. Greenleaf, *Servant Leadership: A Journey into the Nature of Legitimate Power and Greatness* 25th Anniversary edition (Mahwah, NJ: Paulist Press, 2002).

6. Marcus Buckingham and Donald O. Clifton, *Now Discover Your Strengths* (New York: The Free Press, 2001).

7. Ibid.

8. Psalm 90:17, author's paraphrase.

9. Susan Headden, "Two Guys and a Dream," *U.S. News & World Report,* February 20, 2006.

10. Ibid.

Chapter Four

1. James Collins, *Good to Great,* (New York: Harper Business, 2001).

2. Sun Tzu, *The Art of War,* ed. James Clavell (New York: Dell Publishing, 1983).

Chapter Five

1. Psalm 25:21, The Holy Bible, New International Version® (Grand Rapids: Zondervan) © 1973, 1978, 1984 by International Bible Society.

2. Associated Press, "Enron founder Ken Lay dies of heart disease," MSNBC, July 5, 2006, htttp://msnbc.msn.com/id/13715925.

3. MSNBC News Services, "Lay, Skilling guilty on nearly all counts," MSNBC, May 25, 2006, http://msnbc.msn.com/id/12968481.

4. Cathy Booth Thomas, "The Enron Effect," *Time,* June 5, 2006.

5. "Enron Statement of Human Rights Principles," http://www.enron.com/corp/pressroom/responsibility/human _rights_statement.html. Note: Author has printed screen shots of this and other postings from this former Enron Web site. With the demise of the company, this material is no longer available online.

6. Bill Mears, "Arthur Anderson Conviction Overturned," CNN.com, May 31, 2005, http://www.cnn.com/2005/LAW/05/31/scotus .arthur.andersen.

7. Barbara Lee Toffler and Jennifer Reingold, *Final Accounting: Ambition, Greed and the Fall of Arthur Andersen* (New York: Broadway Books, 2003).

8. Derek Kidner, *Proverbs* (Downers Grove, IL: InterVarsity Press, 1964).

9. Devin Leonard, "All I Want in Life Is An Unfair Advantage," *Fortune,* August 8, 2005.

10. Stanley Weiser and Oliver Stone, (screenwriters), *Wall Street* (20th Century Fox, 1987).

11. Lorrie Grant, "RadioShack CEO Quits Over Items on Résumé," *USA Today*, February 21, 2006.

12. Wikipedia.org, s.v. Rosie Ruiz, en.wikipedia.org/wiki/Rosie_Ruiz.

Chapter Seven

1. Daniel Kadlec, "Does Kozlowski's Sentence Fit the Crime?" *Time,* September 20, 2005.

2. "Kozlowski, Tyco face more questions," CNNMoney.com, August 7, 2002, http://money.cnn.com/2002/08/07/news/companies /tyco_kozlowski.

3. Dean Foust and Nanette Byrnes, "Gone Flat," *Business Week,* December 20, 2004.

4. Adam Levy and Steve Matthews, "Coke's World of Woes," *Bloomberg Markets,* July 2004.

5. B. McKay, N. Deogun, and J. Lublin, "Clumsy Handling of Many Problems Cost Ivester Coca-Cola Board's Favor," *Wall Street Journal,* December 17, 1999.

Chapter Eight

1. Sharon E. Epperson, Lawrence Mondi, James L. Graft, and Lisa H. Towle, "EQ," *Time,* October 2, 2005.

2. Daniel Goleman, *Emotional Intelligence* (New York, Bantam Books, 1994).

3. Martin Seligman, *Learned Optimism: How to Change Your Mind and Your Life* (The Free Press, 1998).

4. Aristotle, *The Nicomachean Ethics,* J.A.K. Thompson, translator, revised by Hugh Tredennick (New York: Penguin Classics, 2003).

5. James 1:19, The Holy Bible, New International Version® (Grand Rapids: Zondervan) © 1973, 1978, 1984 by International Bible Society.

6. "Growing Leadership for the Twenty-First Century," A. MacMillan (Atlanta, GA: Team Resources, Inc., 2005).

7. James 3:4–5, The Holy Bible, New International Version® (Grand Rapids: Zondervan) © 1973, 1978, 1984 by International Bible Society.

Chapter Nine

1. Proverbs 18:13, The Message by Eugene H. Peterson (Colorado, Springs: NavPress Publishing Group) Copyright © 1993, 1994, 1995, 1996, 2000, 2001, 2002.

2. Everett Worthington, *Five Steps to Forgiveness: The Art and Science of Forgiving,* (New York: Crown Publishers, 2001).

Chapter Ten

1. "Winner," interview with Tom Brady (Steve Kroft, cohost), *60 Minutes*, November 6, 2005.

2. Sun Tzu, *The Art of War*, ed. James Clavell (New York: Dell Publishing, 1983).

3. Benjamin Franklin, *The Complete Poor Richard Almanacks*, 1758, facsimile edition, vol. 2 (The Imprint Society, 1970), 375.

4. T.S. Eliot (1888–1965), poet, dramatist, literary critic.

5. Thinkexist.com, s.v. Hesiod, en.thinkexist.com/quotes/hesiod.

Chapter Eleven

1. Gregory Allen Howard (screenwriter), *Remember the Titans*, (Walt Disney Pictures, 2000).

2. Walt Kelly, *Pogo* strip for Earth Day 1971 © 1971, 2005 OGPI, from Wikipedia.org, http://en.wikipedia.org/wiki/Pogo.

3. V. E. Frankl, *Man's Search for Meaning* (Boston: Beacon Press, 2000).

4. Brainyquote.com, s.v. Helen Keller, www.brainyquote.com /quotes/authors/h/helen_keller.html.

Epilogue

1. Lawrence Crabb, *The Silence of Adam* (Grand Rapids: Zondervan, 1995).

2. M. Scott Peck, *The Road Less Traveled* (New York: Touchstone/Simon & Schuster, 1978).

3. Steve Forbes, "A Tribute to Peter Drucker," *Wall Street Journal*, November 15, 2005.

4. Hebrews 12:1, The Living Bible (Wheaton, Illinois: Tyndale House Publishers, 1971).

5. C. S. Lewis, *The Chronicles of Narnia: The Last Battle* (New York: Harper Trophy/Harper Collins Publishers, 1956).

About the Author

Dr. Tim Irwin has consulted for more than twenty years with many of America's most well-known and respected companies, including a number of the Fortune 500. He is a frequent speaker on leadership development and other topics related to organizational effectiveness.

Tim has assisted corporations in diverse industries, including fiber optics, real estate, financial services, baby products, information technologies, news and entertainment, insurance, hotels, high-technology research, chemicals, floor covering, bottling, quick service restaurants, fibers and textiles, electronics, and pharmaceuticals. He served for a number of years as the facilitator of the Regional Leadership Institute in Atlanta. His work has taken him to more than twenty-five countries in Europe, Latin America, Canada, and Asia.

Tim worked from 2000 to 2005 in senior management of a firm with more than 300 offices worldwide, specializing in organizational effectiveness, talent management, and leadership development. He has served on both for-profit and nonprofit boards and is currently managing partner of IrwinInc.

Tim received his A.B. and M.A. degrees from the University of Georgia in Athens. His Ph.D. training included a dual major in industrial/ organizational and clinical psychology from Georgia State University in Atlanta. He is a licensed psychologist and an adjunct professor of psychology at the University of Georgia and at Reformed Theological Seminary in Orlando, Florida.

Tim started "running with the bulls" at age 10. He has worked in a number of different jobs, including lawn maintenance, shoe salesman, men's clothing salesman, newspaper ad salesman, construction worker, entertainment critic, cafeteria worker, lifeguard, lab administrator, college professor, counselor, entrepreneur, manager/ leader, consultant, and writer.

Tim and his wife, Anne, live in Atlanta, Georgia and have two married sons. Tim's outside interests include golf, fishing, and scuba diving.

Run Smarter.
Find More Resources Online.

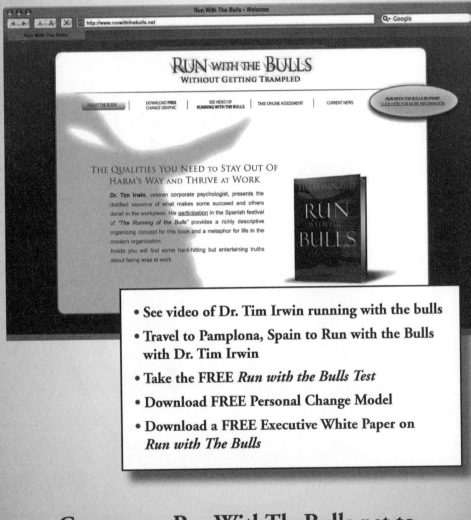

- See video of Dr. Tim Irwin running with the bulls
- Travel to Pamplona, Spain to Run with the Bulls with Dr. Tim Irwin
- Take the FREE *Run with the Bulls Test*
- Download FREE Personal Change Model
- Download a FREE Executive White Paper on *Run with The Bulls*

Go to www.RunWithTheBulls.net to download your FREE resources.

Can You Run Without
Getting Trampled?

Go Online to Find Out
at www.RunWithTheBulls.net.